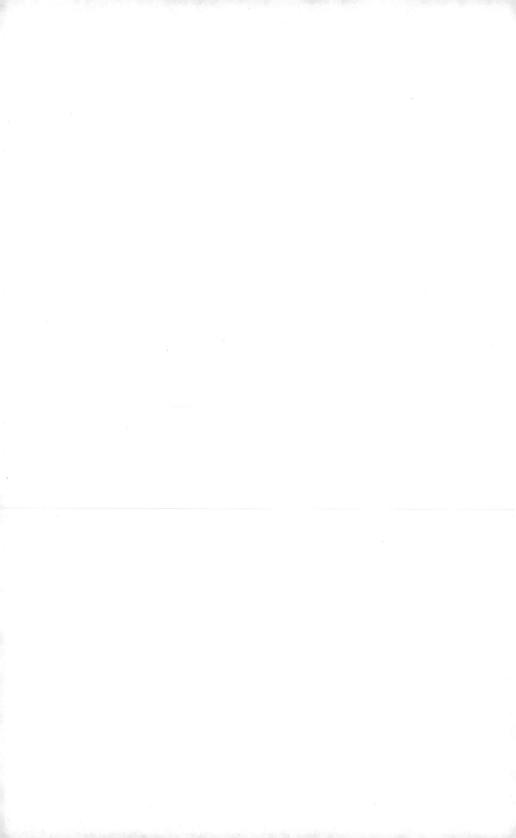

THE HUMANITIES:

the other side of the river?

The Proceedings of the 1967

Cranbrook Curriculum Conference

on

The Humanities

RICHARD E. STARKEY, *Editor*

MARCIA D. STARKEY, *Bibliographer*

We wish to acknowledge the cooperation of the following publishers in granting permission to quote from their publications:

To Harper & Row for the "Lit Instructor"
Stafford, William; *Traveling through the Dark.*
Harper & Row, New York, 1962.

To The Macmillan Company for "The Man He Killed"
Hardy, Thomas; *The Collected Poems of
Thomas Hardy.*
Macmillan, New York, 1926

C B
3
.C 7
1967

TABLE OF CONTENTS

41901

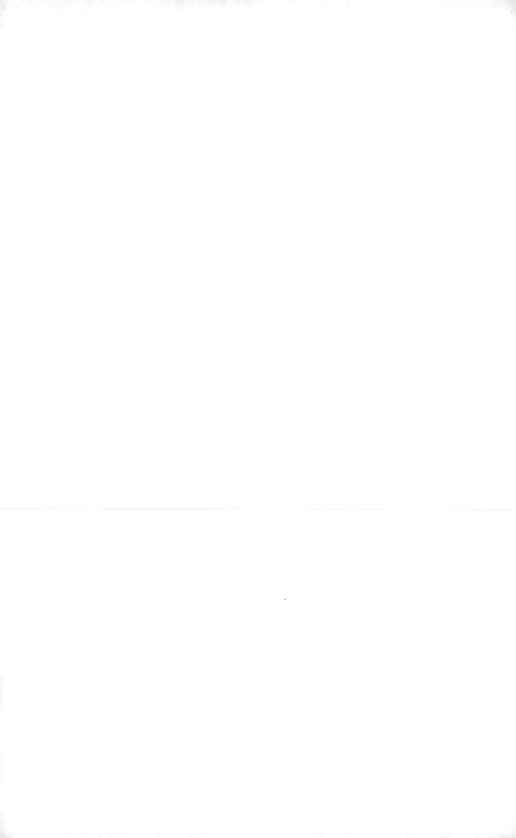

WHAT IS CRANBROOK?

CRANBROOK, in Bloomfield Hills, Michigan, is a cultural and educational center occupying three hundred acres.

The six institutions of Cranbrook, located on a common campus and independently governed by their own boards, are the gift of George G. Booth, Michigan newspaper publisher, and his wife, Ellen Scripps Booth.

Brookside School Cranbrook
Kingswood School Cranbrook for Girls
Cranbrook School for Boys
Cranbrook Academy of Art and Galleries
Cranbrook Institute of Science
Christ Church Cranbrook

WHAT IS THE CRANBROOK CURRICULUM CONFERENCE?

AN OPPORTUNITY for elementary and secondary school educators to hear first hand the current debate from the people who create nation-wide trends.

An opportunity for public, parochial and independent personnel to share their common interests and concerns, to strengthen the community which they all serve and to recognize the variety of approaches possible in American education.

The Conference is one of the functions of the Cranbrook Curriculum Center. The Center, located in Cranbrook House in Bloomfield Hills, Michigan, maintains a continuous program of acquiring new teaching materials, publishers' information and curriculum guides. All of the materials listed in bibliographies accompanying this publication and previous publications are available for examination at the Center.

Prior Publications

REVOLUTION & REACTION: *the impact of the new social studies.*
© 1966.

OUT OF PRINT

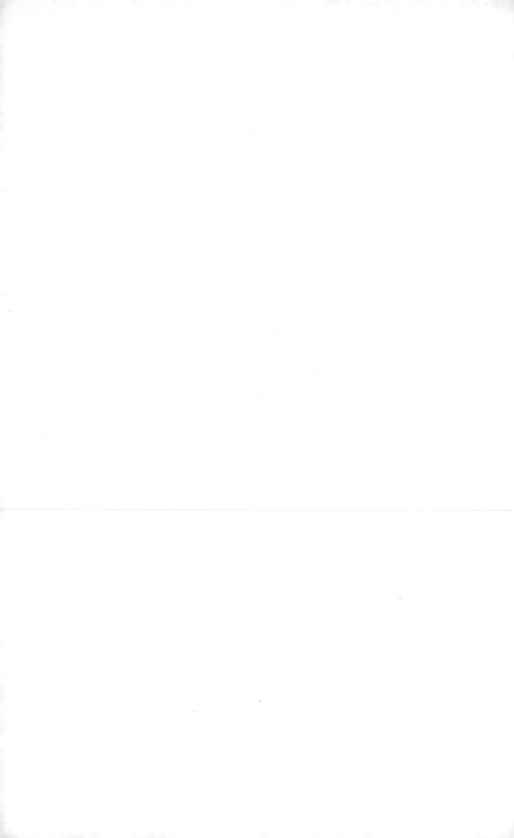

PREFACE

THIS volume is the second in a series of conference proceedings. It was the intention of the organizers of the Cranbrook Curriculum Conference to produce, in published form, the speeches and discussion of the conference. We acknowledge, with deep thanks and appreciation, those who helped bring this current volume into existence.

We especially acknowledge the contributions of our speakers who have supplied copies of or corrected tape scripts of their speeches. We wish to acknowldge the services of Marcia D. Starkey, in supplying the bibliography; Jeanette Maloney for transcribing the tapes of the sessions and Norma C. Anderson for her editorial assistance.

To our colleagues of the Cranbrook Institutions who made valuable suggestions and assisted in the Conference, we also give our thanks.

ת

PROLOGUE

THE Humanities are in a state of ferment. As has been the case in the past, the nature, role and function of this ancient academic concern is undergoing redefinition. It may be that the full attainment of an adequate, comprehensive definition of the Humanities is, like Promised Land, always across the river. A Jordan, deep with our singular prejudices and wider than our narrow range of vision. We do not claim for this volume any magic boat which will span the river—but we do hope to provide some insights for those who are looking for a more adequate way to approach the Humanistic concerns.

In *1787: The Grand Convention* Clinton Rossiter gives his justification for study of the event, the constitutional convention. "Even if all historians were to agree—the most unlikely of occurrences—on the 'truth' of each of the thousands of episodes, discussions . . . they would still be left with the larger meaning of the happening for the men of their own generation. And since each generation . . . has its own problems and aspirations, its 'rendezvous with destiny' unlike that of any other generation, the scholars of each must be prepared to think about (it) as if it had never been thought about at all".

Rossiter's justification for the re-study of the Grand Convention applies, equally, to the Humanities. Dean Matthews, in his presentation herein, essayed the varied shape of the Humanities through the years. As we follow changing outlines of the scholastic metes and bounds, it becomes clear that each generation of humanists has re-studied and re-defined the nature and scope of the Humanities. Pre-eminently the humanists have, as Matthews indicates, been "convinced of the efficacy of literature as a civilizing influence."

We have not, in case there is any question, evolved the ultimate definition of the nature of the Humanities—we have attempted to suggest ways in which the separate academic disciplines contribute toward making man more truly human. We have perhaps suggested working definitions by outlining the negative—what the "Humanities are not."

11

We have of necessity posited a working definition. A definition which is *tentative* and incomplete. We have assumed that what constitutes the Humanities is basically a "spirit," an approach to a subject. It is not to be confused with classicism or art and music appreciation—although too often in order to be "up-to-date" some of our schools have gathered these traditional but not necessarily humane subjects under a catalog listing as the Humanities Department.[1]

If we assume that the Humanities are best characterized by the quest for those things which most contribute to making man more truly human, we can evolve a viable, albeit pragmatic, framework for what follows. It is then possible for any teacher to create an overriding humanistic framework or structure for any course he or she may teach.

Much of our classroom work involves exposing the student to the tools of a discipline: the vocabularly, methodology or teachings germaine to the field. The teacher, in attempting to give an understanding of his subject matter, often falls into the trap of emphasizing the analytic tools of the discipline and the data accumulated by the profession to the point where these become the end of his teaching. The music teacher who stresses accumulation of music skills—rhythm, tempo, chord structure, etc.—is shortchanging himself and his students if he doesn't ask "how does the music say? what does it mean to you? what does it say about the human condition, at the time of its composition —now?" This latter is really what the Humanities are about— what *is* the human condition and *how can* we become a more significant person.

If we can accept this as our working definition of the Humanities we can open the door to any teacher, any discipline, including or perhaps especially the sciences and welcome them to the Humanities fold. By the nature of the academic beast we have focused an art, music, literature and history, which are most often associated with the Humanities. We could have

---

[1]William Arrowsmith, "The Shame of the Graduate Schools," *Harper's*, Vol. 232, March, 1966, p. 51.

included many more subjects with equal justification. We would suggest that for future exploration we enter into a dialogue with our colleagues, exploring the Humanistic base of all learning, rather than the interminable discussion of grading systems and the discipline problems. But this happy land will always be —the other side of the river.

THE HUMANITIES AND THE SCHOOLS

HAROLD TAYLOR

THE AMERICAN poet William Jay Smith, in a review of the work of several young American poets, pointed out that culture with a capital "C" is being organized in America on a very large scale and that the concern of the people had turned to cultural matters. This, said Mr. Smith, was shown by the fact that the Government had become interested, Congress had passed legislation and the President of the United States had recognized its existence by inviting distinguished intellects to his inauguration. As they went from their hotels to the inauguration itself, they were taken there in a bus on which was the sign "Cultural Leaders."

I am intrigued by Mr. Smith's remarks about the organization of big culture and the organization of big cultural leaders who travel in buses, especially as this has to do with the universities and schools. The universities have, as you know, taken hold of the organization of knowledge at large and organized the delight right out of it. The students who enroll in this organization are fed the grist from the academic mill and the successful scholar is now a promoter-organizer.

It is just possible that the educators, given the slightest encouragement, will organize the daylights out of the arts in exactly the same way that they have in the case of the sciences and social studies. In fact, the university, when looked at precisely, now has the characteristics of a cultural bus with bus drivers more interested in the financing of the bus company and the horsepower of the engine than in whether the passengers are on the right bus or have any clear idea of where they are going. Mr. Smith called attention to this conception of culture because at the time he was reviewing the poets he had found university presses publishing their own poets and their own poetry books. He had found, as we all do, poets lecturing and reading their poems to large university audiences, and that the slim volumes of earlier years had been replaced by fatter volumes full of poems, in Mr. Smith's term, "conspicuously unedited."

The result of the involvement of the universities with poetry, Mr. Smith implied, is the production of more poems but less poetry. This seems to me to be the problem of the arts in relation to what are now called the humanities, whether we are talking about them in the universities or anywhere else. How to organize on a large scale for a mass culture these most precious values within the human community, without killing them off or maiming them forever. There are always practical arrangements to be made. Someone has to get the chairs into the auditorium, the lectern on the platform, the money for the fees, the buildings for the arts. When all this was a matter in the universities and in some private schools of one or two eccentrics in the faculty who read little magazines and knew who the new poets, composers and writers were, there was no problem, since there were so few readers of or listeners to poetry in the colleges and since so few poems and absolutely no plays were ever written on any campus. There were no playwrights, painters or other such people teaching there.

Now there is a problem because the cultural leaders all have names and the names are known, respected, admired and wanted. The arts also have names that are known and respected. We have not yet learned what to do with the arts and the artists within a capitalist society and a democratic culture where the worth of things is so commonly judged by their capacity to attract money and the things most worth judging are not often financially attractive. It is now clear to me that there is no other place than the schools and the colleges for the arts to find a home. There is no more natural place for their home to be.

I say this out of the experience of being president of the American Ballet Theater Foundation and finding to my astonishment that the more successful a ballet company becomes the more money it loses, until we now have managed to demonstrate the quality of our work by losing $700,000 a year. We not only lose more money per square foot of performance than any other ballet company, but we have a wider repertory with which to lose it. I bring to you also direct experience with the

Martha Graham Company, where we don't quite lose so much money, but we explore the problem of the contemporary artist in society by an annual scrutiny of whether or not we will be able to perform again in the coming season.

It is an irony that Miss Graham, whose work has without question made the greatest contribution to dance theater in the western world in the last forty years, had not toured the United States in eighteen years until this past year when the United States Government, through the National Endowment for the Arts, made that possible by a grant of $150,000. The supreme irony that Miss Graham and her art and that form of human expression represented by a truly native American art form, which drew its energies from an entire world of art in every other culture, was seen abroad every other year or so but had not been seen in the United States. I draw attention to William Joy Smith's analogy and the growth of big culture and big organizations for culture to juxtapose this with the problems of developing artists and their work. This points to the exact center of our problem in the field of American education.

We have on the one hand an extraordinary set of advances in the interest of American society in the art forms of the West. It is extraordinary advance in the interests of people who even ten years ago had much less concern for the arts or what is commonly called culture, but who through the impact of the mass media and the double impact of the mass media coupled with a new middle class able to purchase works of art or to have something to do with art—have moved the cultural organizations ahead while creating the economic and aesthetic problem of what to do with the arts in a mass society. As you are probably aware, from last year's figures there were 1,401 symphony orchestras in the United States, 40,000 theater organizations, 754 opera groups, 200 dance groups and upwards of $500,000,000 a year spent in admissions to dance, theater and musical performances. More than 100 bills about the arts have been introduced into Congress over the past five years; more than 40 new Arts Councils have been established in the past two years in the states around the country.

The difficulty is not merely economic, but it is a question of how we can support the live center from which all the arts must flow. This is the real question, and this brings us to the schools. There has been an enormous impact of popular interest in culture. What we can honestly refer to as a mass culture has developed, comprised of the popular arts of television, the paperback book, the spread of the news magazine, the weekly magazine which pays attention to the arts with quite superb reproductions and art criticism, the spread of the little theater movement, community theater, dance, painting, the spread of museums as centers for educational work rather than as mausoleums, an entirely new feeling has entered.

I would like to tackle one sector of that for a moment before going on to the relationship between what I have to say and its educational implications for schools. As the concern of the American people has grown for a share in their cultural heritage and in the heritage of the Western arts at large, we have again applied a characteristically American approach to the way in which we have begun to organize the arts. I am referring to the phenomenon of the cultural center which is seen as its most monstrous in New York City, and where we have what is called Lincoln Center where we do our best to put the arts out of business by making them so expensive that only those with money can go. It also segregates into one huge block some mixed architecture for around 10,000 people at once, and therefore makes it impossible to get to any one of the performances, or to get home from it.

This has become a national solution to the problem of the arts. I refer you to one of our most penetrating critics of popular art and of social process in the United States, Jules Feiffer, the cartoonist who has now turned playwright. Art has become a social asset, he says. "We can create light bulbs and bottle caps on one side, poets and painters on the other, but what we cannot and have not created is a prevailing sense of culture—an atmosphere in which the individual arts are not only allowed to endure against the tide, but to grow. All true, except for the fact that in our utilitarian art we seem to have reached the point of no return where telephones have been invented that can't be dialed, beer cans that can't be opened and jobs that require no people. The corresponding step in the creative field is to invent cultural centers that have no culture,—a logical maneuver in the growth of the only social art we have yet discovered;—it is self-destruction.

The concept of the concentrated cultural zoo, divorced neatly from our real lives, is an increasingly popular one. While the rest of our landscape uglies up, we are anxious to build a place (*some*place) that is pretty, an official pretty, a pretty we can go to, pay a dollar to, come home from and say, "Yes, I have seen pretty. It is there." The more ugly life gets outside our windows, the more anxious we are to contain beauty elsewhere; a tree inside a fence, a bird inside a sanctuary, an artist inside a zoo. Aware of our impulse mainly to destroy, we cage those things we think it desirable to save. What we leave on the outside is show business, portraits of lonely artists discussing their alienation in full color picture books or with David Suskind on television.

Mr. Feiffer then goes on to say that he doesn't object to the massive increase in official art, since if there is art of any kind and if it is produced on a massive scale by more and more painters, sculptors, playwrights and the others, we are bound to have a kind of fallout from all this activity, and something good may eventually happen. Mr. Feiffer is not objecting to the proliferation of a mass culture. He is drawing attention to the central point to be taken into consideration when we talk about what to do with the arts in America.

As we look at the history of American education over these past 25 years, we will see a shift towards a conservative point of view—not merely about the arts but about those aspects of human life which are so directly involved in and with the arts that is to say, the moral, aesthetic, political and social issues of a society. What we have managed to do during the 25 years is so successfully to segregate the moral, aesthetic and political issues from the actual work of the colleges and universities that in order to become sensitive to the major issues of contemporary society, it is better not to be in school or in college. If one is in college as a student, one can occasionally catch a glimpse of issues which are agonizing mankind and the world, but only if one does this on one's own, like organizing a demonstration against the President, or organizing teach-ins on the Vietnam war, thus raising the only serious political and moral issues which are ever raised on the campus.

An intensity of concern for the issues of war and peace, ugliness and beauty, truth and falsehood, is at the heart of what we should be referring to as the humanities. But a keen look at the recent history of American education will show the gradually flattening-out process by which we have managed to squash all issues and turn the curriculum into a series of academic subjects taught by academic experts to students who are considered passive recipients of what is known among academic experts. I will not take your time to provide you with the standard indictment, which is now fairly well distributed in the literature of some who have made a career out of denunciation. Let me simply say what is obviously true, that what is called culture in the colleges is now a concentrated cultural zoo in which the subject matter of the humanities is assumed to have captured the insights of the human race and is able to dispense these insights at three credits a throw by the lecture system and is able by a miraculous process to grade the ability to understand the human spirit up to three decimal points.

This is obviously an absurd way of treating the human mind and human experience, but it is done every day, all day, all over the country. The real issue is, how can we bring to the American student body, both in the schools and in the colleges, the spirit of humanism, the spirit of the human race at its best, and raise the level of sensitivity of the students to the real issues in contemporary life and in the life of man in the past. I submit to you that the way we are now dealing with it is exactly the way *not* to do it. It may be that I am not the right person to speak at the beginning of this conference, since my conception of the humanities is so widely different from that practiced in most universities and schools. What I have to say, while being the absolute truth, is contrary to what is popularly assumed to be true. But as I go along I will try to be fair to others who are so wrong-headed.

Let me look for a moment at the tendency to capture objects and to build buildings before one thinks of the creative process by which true objects of art are brought into existence. It is an unfortunate fact that with such constellations of architecture as Lincoln Center, we actually have no new plays to put into them. We have not very much new music being written that is worthy of buildings of such extraordinary size. I cite two examples: in the Lincoln Center Repertory Theater there were only two plays in three years which commanded the serious attention of critics and of the public alike both by Arthur Miller.

Sam Barber's opera was a social success and an aesthetic failure, and the opening of the new Metropolitan Opera House at Lincoln Center celebrated the absence of great American operatic talent. It was a good opera with a horse on the stage, one of the most elaborate stage sets you could see anywhere, but it was not a contribution to the literature of dramatic theater, musical theater or opera in the western world.

We have not solved the problem. The artist as outsider, and the cultural entrepreneur as insider, this gives us the problem of developing a lively critical and creative body of persons whose ideas flow daily from their own concerns, that is the problem we have to be dealing with in the educational system. When we look at the question of developing the sensibility of the young, we would be well advised if we did not try to develop that sensibility by the kind of courses and the kind of attitudes to education which have grown up in what is an extraordinarily conservative educational community in the United States. The conception of education as the dispensing of academic materials has now become so common that it is very difficult to get educators thinking or talking about education in any other terms than courses, textbooks, anthologies, lectures, academic credits.

21

I have just been through an exhausting year looking at the education of teachers in the United States with particular attention to their education in the field of world affairs. I have, therefore, visited classes with the students, taught fourth grade classes and high school classes and watched other people teach them. I have been to class with the education students, with the students of arts and sciences in the undergraduate and graduate schools; I have taught undergraduate and graduate classes; I have listened to deans and presidents; I have talked back to them and conferred with them; I have talked to college of education faculty members and to regulation arts and science departmental knowledge-dispensers; and I know what I mean when I say that the sterilizing effect of the present under-graduate instruction in America is so great that any student who has a spark of interest in the arts and the humanities in connection with his college education can have that spark completely obliterated by the time he gets through one of the courses in the humanities which are now required in so many colleges across the country.

What you have in these courses is usually—and I am not caricaturing them; I am choosing my words very carefully—is an anthology with bits of knowledge drawn from the re-spectable thinkers of the western world, a few poets, a few literary critics, put together in a humanities survey course on the assumption that this will give the student a conception of his own cultural background. It is not merely a Great Books' approach, but it is bits from books that are considered to be great. I submit to you that this is the fastest way to kill the interest of a student in books in general and thinking and thinkers in particular.

The way in which one needs to develop the sensitivity of the student to the values in human society, to the arts as they are practiced, is to give the student a chance to go sufficiently deeply into the areas of life which art artist, the writer, the philosopher, the humanist inhabits, so that the student can understand what that kind of person is like, so that he can come close to the reality of the experience of the poet, the philosopher and of those who generate the values which then are put in the courses called the humanities.

My point might be made by distinguishing between the two National Endowments for the arts and the humanities. If you look at the debates in Congress and around the country at the time the legislation for an Arts Council and Humanities Council was first proposed, you will find two basic arguments. The first argument is that since the sciences and the technologies have been supported by the United States Government, by industry, by the university, by everyone else, that, therefore, the humanities—the counterpart of the sciences—should have their day. We should be supporting them too, otherwise we will not be wise enough to use our technologies. The second argument is that no person who graduates from school or college should be ignorant of his own heritage in the humanities and the arts and that therefore, we need to rectify that situation.

Then the question came: If we are going to have a National Council on the Arts, what do we do about the humanities? The practicing artists and the critics who were close to the practicing artists, immediately formed a solid phalanx against the notion that artists should have anything to do with the humanities. Their feeling was that the academic scholars would take all the money and use it in the universities—they would destroy the arts with the speed of light. The humanities were accordingly separated from the arts.

If you have been following the matter closely, you will know that there is a National Endowment for the Arts which gives money, for example, to the American Ballet Theater and to Martha Graham; and, on the other hand, there is the National Endowment for the Humanities which, when last seen, was giving grants for bibliographies in medieval history and scholarly research in corners of the arts. I am not here to deny the value of having money spent for that, but if you look at the list of grants, it can be seen that almost every foundation that ever gave money away to anything has already given money to the things now supported by the Endowment. This represents in dramatic form, in institutional form, in political form, what I mean to say about the relation of the arts to the humanities.

I believe that the arts themselves are the source of the entire spirit of the humanities and that when you divorce the practice of an art from its criticism its history, from the ongoing discussion about it, you destroy the art itself. You make very unlikely the possibility that the student you are teaching will ever quicken his imagination or his aesthetic sensitivity to the art simply by hearing about it. The source of knowledge in the arts and in the humanities is in the artist and in what he is saying about life, the interpretation he is giving of the world he sees as a painter, as a sculptor, or the world as imagined by the playwright, the poet, the novelist. These are the things which must lie at the heart of the humanities in the schools. The anthological approach to putting the humanities into an academic system is quite likely to spoil the entire enterprise as far as the students are concerned.

Herbert Read has a phrase to describe what I mean. Read is devoted to the notion that education through the arts is the primary education which can open up whole areas of knowledge to the student's mind and he urges that we should make more intense the natural perceptions of the human being. The aesthetic element in all learning is the involvement of the student in the act of learning and until the student has had an active experience with one of the arts, he has not begun to learn about them. It is the primary movement in consciousness toward the thing being learned to which we should be giving our attention. Our role as teachers in the humanities must be to make more intense the natural perceptions of reality which we already have.

What then do we do in the schools?

I would suggest rather practical things. I would suggest we pay attention to how teachers are being developed. Unless what we are going to do is to produce foolproof curricula, which is what the textbook manufacturers say cynically—a teacher-proof curriculum, one which even a dummy can teach—we are going to have to pay much, much more attention to how we are educating teachers in the arts.

There is a relation here between the arts and the world in which they occur. If one thinks of a sensitivity to the issues in world society, one will obviously be thinking of the capacity for response, for example, to the horrors of war or to victims of famine. One's moral imagination needs to become sufficiently sensitive to recognize the difficulties of the human race in parts of the world unlike one's own. Whether we want to sensitize our students to moral and world issues or aesthetic and art issues, we are concerned with the imagination.

When you look at the teaching of music in the American public schools you find that music is, of all the arts, the one most commonly taught. In some school systems, as in Boston, you have 60,000 young people playing instruments, singing and actually studying music at a level of proficiency which makes the art form understandable to them. But in most parts of the country the 50,000 bands which now exist are playing for football and basketball games some of the most absurd music to be found. Why? Because we are back to the concept of segregated culture. Culture is something you have in a museum, what is done by the Metropolitan Opera or by a ballet company, whereas what you do in the school is produce things for athletic events—football and basketball are substitutes for opera and ballet. They are our popular art forms.

When you look at those who are teaching music you find that only 5 percent of all those who are teaching have had serious experience and training in music. They have usually taken one course in music appreciation; they may have played the trumpet in one of those 50,000 bands. The choral director is a man who has certain skills in organization and whose skill does not run to choice of works from the great choral repertory.

This is also true of the art teachers; only about 7 percent of them have ever done any serious work in painting, or sculpture, or in art history.

I am not denying the values of so much of what is happening

by those who are working as artists and as musicians and composers in schools. I am saying that as a national problem we
have not even begun to think about it in the correct terms. That
is to say, one cannot have great art in society unless there is an
institutional base through which the art can come. American
society is now demanding more of the arts, while in the schools
we are still dumbling in trivial ways to educate teachers to
teach the humanities and the arts themselves.

We then must ask, where do we get the teachers from? When
we look at what is happening in the colleges, we find that in
certain of them, for example, the Music Conservatory at Ober-
lin, there are fully accomplished musicians. When we look at
the high schools, we can be astonished with the quality of
playing and a musicianship on the part of an increasing number
of high school students who have become devoted to the violin,
the cello, the oboe; all the brass, woodwind instruments. The
accomplishment of some of the young musicians in the colleges
and universities where music is taken seriously gives us hope
that if we used the qualities existing in the present student body
and we thought of teacher training not as training, but as the
opportunity for practicing the arts while learning to teach them,
we could recruit an increasing number of young men and
women interested in dance, theater, music, painting and sculpture. If we simply seized upon the growing amount of interest
on the part of the younger generation in the arts themselves,
and if we constructed our college courses to make these interests
flourish, we could combine this with a lively teacher-education
program. If these young people, while in college, were teaching
in the elementary schools and the high schools in the art form
of their choice, we could create a new attitude both to teacher
education and to the place of the arts in the schools.

Norman Dello Jois, the composer, is in charge of a program
sponsored by the Ford Foundation to place composers in
residence in the American high schools. In the high schools
which have composers there has been in some cases a miraculous transformation of the attitude of the school itself to the
humanities and the arts simply because of the presence of one

composer, who writes for small groups of instruments, then begins to encourage some of the young people who themselves have never written before to write small works for two or three instruments. The first thing you know someone in the school has thought of doing a small opera, and the first thing you know the notion that poetry is a form of sung words begins to creep into the literature department. A lively composer with a talent for teaching can have an enormous impact. We need more teachers who themselves are so committed to an interest in one of the arts that they will respond to the opportunity to teach the art itself.

At Sarah Lawrence College we were concerned that the children in Yonkers and in Mount Vernon nearby were deprived of any contact with live art. The children there are not only intellectually, culturally and economically impoverished, but the school system gives them very little aesthetic nourishment. It therefore seemed appropriate for us to develop a program at the college in which our students could work in the arts and the humanities with the children of Yonkers. We called for volunteers from the students, many of whom volunteered to teach theater, music, dance, and painting to the children of Yonkers on Saturday mornings. Before long the college had developed a children's theater, dance classes for children, and music classes in which seven and eight year olds were composing music with the help of our students. There was percussion music if the children had no instruments, and we produced a kind of new art form—children's percussion—the like of which you have never heard and which I do not recommend to any but the hardiest of souls. We had on the part of our students an extraordinarily flourishing interest in teaching theater, dance and music which could not have been called into action had they not had the experience of teaching children.

Teaching children in the arts is one of the fastest way to encourage the spirit of the humanities in any school or college. To work with children in the arts you have to strip down what you are doing to the most honest and integral form of art, since the children are such devastating critics. They do not have to stay in the room and be polite during a performance. If they do not like something, it shows immediately. It is not that they necessarily dislike actively the art being presented, it is simply that they cannot sustain attention to something which to them is aesthetically invalid. I can recall vividly some of the works which our students did in collaboration with children and for children. They were valid works of art which could not have been done except through the relationship of teaching children. I can recall one opera written by a Sarah art student on the theme of a princess who talked backwards—an interesting speech impediment for anyone who intended to become a queen, and it bothered the king and the queen that she was backward in this particular sense. The student had composed the score for dancers, actors, a chorus, an orchestra, with 50 to 60 students from the college involved in an opera which was not only engaging as a work by a student in college, but a work of art for children. It was enhanced by the fact that it was written for children. That student is now a teacher of the humanities in a public school system in Westchester and is bringing the force of her intelligence and creative energies to work on the problem of teaching the arts in the schools of Westchester.

We must first of all pay attention to how we are going to develop teachers who are able to make their own curricula, to compose, to paint, to act as living examples of persons concerned with aesthetic values—not simply dispensers of second-hand information of what other artists have done and have said. The distinction which we commonly make between vocational and liberal education tends to put the humanities to one side with the liberal and consider the arts as part of a vocation or profession. This is also seen in the teacher-education courses where the practice of teaching is considered as a necessary duty performed in order to get a certificate. To me teaching is an exciting form of liberal education especially teaching children in the arts. If we think of the humanities and their connection to the rest of human experience as being one of continuity rather than of discrete entities, we would arrange, in an ideal college where teachers for the humanities were being prepared, that students could listen to a record of Dylan

Thomas reading his own poem, "Do not go Gentle into that Good Night." This would be a shared experience of poetry by students in the presence of a poet, not an exercise in how to use the gramaphone to teach poetry. It would be a shared experience of the poem.

Similarly, the student who works with children in the field of poetry would not be practicing teaching except by indirection. The student would be learning how poetic is the child's mind, what natural storytellers and poets and writers and painters and sculptors they are, and what interesting work they do when given a chance. The student learning to teach poetry is learning what it is like to be a child in the presence of poetry. The imagery and the insights of the children furnish the material for the student's own education.

I suggest that we must break down the notion that in developing young people who are interested in teaching the humanities we must send them out to practice teaching in order to dispense the information they get in humanities courses back on the campus. That is not the way it works. The experience of the art form itself, the participation in it, is the crucial element. In learning to teach the art, you are learning the art itself.

I also suggest that we must revise quite thoroughly what we consider to be appropriate things for high school students to read. The more astute and sophisticated of them have already been through a wide number of paperbacks, which when I was a boy did not exist. A book to me was something that the librarians held and tried to keep away from you. If you did manage to get one away from them, they wanted it back in about two hours. The difficulty in the college humanities courses, as well as in the high school courses, is reading against deadlines and reading small sections, up to page 72½ by next Friday. There is a dutiful scheduled arrangement in the reading assignments themselves.

Reading, if it is to be fully educational, if it is to touch the core of the matter as far as the arts and the humanities are concerned, must be reading which is enjoyed and felt. Without the enjoyment the education is not happening. If you want to know what has happened, in the newspaper reader's sense, then you can read without enjoyment. But if it is a matter of nourishing your own sensibility in the humanities, the question of enjoyment and intensity of experience is paramount. Without that intensity of perception and of engagement with the work itself, it is educationally valueless. We therefore have to be quite precise in the choice of works to which the students can bring an appropriate response. This means that at the beginning, we may wish to bring them works which do not have respectability in the classical repertory. Just as for young dancers, it is ridiculous to start them off dancing in Swan Lake, before they have managed to find out how to get on their toes, so with the standard classics of western literature, the question is whether or not it is something which at this moment in time these particular students are capable of responding to. The notion that only works which are well known and highly advertised with names like Plato attached to them, can be read and still educate, needs to be dismissed. We need to think of the entire range of films, of paperbacks, of possible theater presentations of a variety of kinds if we are going to take seriously the construction of new courses in the humanities. Some of the most fascinating new developments in the teaching of the humanities in the colleges have come from the young film makers, who through the experience of spending six months working on a 15-minute film, have achieved an intensity of perception about the arts and, therefore, about the humanities which is almost impossible to achieve by the usual media, even by writing a play. I believe that as a form of teacher training for the arts and the humanities, making a film is one of the most valuable with which to experiment. Those of you who have seen some of the young film makers' films will realize the truth of what I am saying.

One of the obstacles to the practice of the arts in the schools is the schedule, which leaves no blocks of time of sufficient length to devote to theater, music, dance, painting and sculpture. If the arts are to be practiced in the high school, they can't be pushed off to weekends, they can't be made peripheral; they must be made central to the schedule in periods longer than 45 minutes. In theater and dance, two and three hour sessions are essential.

Another of the difficulties is to find sufficient time for the teachers to deal with the interest in art which the students themselves, once they are stirred up, insist on continuing. We must get used to the fact that the student body can be made in many ways, self-teaching. That is to say, some of the most gifted of the high school and college students are perfectly capable of doing the teaching and supervision necessary to continue the kind of teaching which is started by an effective teacher. We should explore in a much more radical way than we ever have before the teaching talents in the student body itself. We should consider our students in terms of what talent they have as potential teachers, turn them loose on teaching assignments, give them the time and the support they need for such assignments.

I will conclude by reading a poem by William Stafford, a man who grew up in the Midwest, attended the University of Kansas, and learned to love and write poetry in the process. He is now teaching literature at Lewis and Clark College in Portland, Oregon. The poem is entitled, "Lit Instructor."[*]

> Day after day, up there beating my wings
> with all of the softness truth requires
> I feel them shrug whenever I pause:
> they class my voice among tentative things,
>
> And they credit fact, force, battering.
> I dance my way toward the family of knowing,
> embracing stray error as a long-lost boy
> and bringing him home with my fluttering

---

[*]Stafford, William; *Travelling Through the Dark*. Harper & Row, New York. p. 38.

Every quick feather asserts a just claim;
it bites like a saw into white pine.
I communicate right; but explain to the dean—
well, Right has a long and intricate name.

And the saying of it is a lonely thing.

It is true, as Stafford says that the poet's voice is classed among tentative things, that the truth of the artist, the truth taught by the artist, is of a different kind, often misunderstood by those more familiar with fact, force, and battering. But day after day, the task of presenting that truth belongs to us, and if what we are trying to do cannot always be explained to the Dean then, as is the case with all the most important things in life, we will have to go on practicing the arts and honoring them without explanation and without apology for their importance.

▲   ▲   ▲

Q. Dr. Taylor, I sense that you are saying to us advocates of teachers of the arts "Do the same thing that advocates of teachers in the sciences do," that is, exclude all other facets from your thinking much as the professional artists did in this thing that went on at Martha's Vineyard. Is this right?

A. I am arguing that a man who is a scientist should be privileged to go as deeply and as intensively into the field of science as his heart takes him and that if he goes deeply and intensively into it, he is not going to be educated narrowly as a scientist. Quite often the mistake people make in thinking about this balance theory of education is: if you have "x" amount of science taught you, you have to balance it by "x" amount of humanities. Whereas, in terms of the experience I have had in watching people being educated and seeing what happens to them, we have got the whole problem skewed. What we need to do is to think of how we can give the young person who is deeply interested in science a deep and immediate experience at the time he is interested, rather than worrying about the fact that if he studies too much science it will spoil him for everything else. Our most interesting and best scientists are those who started when they were quite young and worked very hard and very deeply in that field and became famous physicists at the age of twenty-six. You can't do that anymore than you can become a ballet dancer without spending hour, after hour, after hour doing the thing you care about.

On the other hand, we don't think of the humanities and the work of the artist in the school in those same terms. We usually think that knowing a little about the history of the art is enough. I am saying that the intensity of experience and involvement in some degree of depth with the art form itself is the ultimate educational factor, just as the involvement with the work in science is the ultimate educational factor. To become a broadly educated person it is first necessary to become deeply interested in one or two things that you care about. The problem for high school students so often is that they have no intellectual interests. I am suggesting the way to develop those intellectual interests and aesthetic interests is to put students to work in one of the arts (or in some aspect of the entire curriculum) in order to stir them up and get them started. I am against the notion of a horizontal approach of something of everything.

There is also something in your question which suggested possibly the need for looking at the existing courses. For example, history is usually taught as a series of wars and political events, which in a sense it is, but that's not terribly interesting. If history is taught from the point of view of the development of persons formed together in clusters at various times in the world's history and various parts of the world and one, say, reads diaries and biographies and studies the history of art and culture in personal terms, then history itself is deeply a part of the arts and humanities; but history as it's usually taught skips the surface of the human concern and simply talks about the public events, acts of parliament and wars. The entire curriculum needs to be looked at as one big humanity or cause, a set of issues which need to be studied.

Q. While I think that participation is perhaps a necessary condition for being a good teacher in this field, is it also a sufficient condition? Is it possible, in other words, to be an artist and still be unable to communicate or to help a student to become a better artist?

A. I'm glad you put it that way because in my over-emphasis on the participation in the art form, I didn't spend as much time as would have been necessary to clear that up. You are absolutely right. There are many artists (and I'm using the term artists as a generic term for people who work in the media of the arts) who are not only unable to communicate but make a point of not. I speak as one who had the responsibility, not to say duty, of appointing artists to the Sarah Lawrence faculty. It's like appointing psychiatrists, if you've ever had that experience. You sit down and interview. Did you ever do that? Sit down and interview a psychiatrist you're thinking of employing? That's a real game. Games college presidents play! To a degree interviewing and deciding about the appointment of an artist to your faculty in a college or high school is a little like that in that some of the really finest young artists that I knew around New York, I couldn't possibly bring into a college, and particularly a college for women. Let me be quite specific. David Smith, an extraordinary man, extraordinarily talented in sculpture, taught at Sarah Lawrence for three years and I deliberately invited him. He was interviewed in a wild pink shirt and a pair of blue jeans, having just come in from Bolton's Landing and the Bolton's Landing Iron Works where he cast his sculpture. Taking a chance on him was something that a high school principal probably wouldn't do since it was very clear there was going to be trouble.

I appointed Randall Jarrell and Mary McCarthy in the same year to Sarah Lawrence with the result that I appeared in American literature as one of the silliest college presidents ever known to man in the two novels, *Pictures from an Institution* and *The Groves of Academe*. Such are the hazards of appointing writers! A high school author will immediately begin writing a novel in which the principal turns out to be an absolute ass. However, placement of compsers and journeymen teachers in high schools, when they're the right ones, have had an extraordinary effect. But it takes a certain kind of person. You have to be a certain kind of musician to be able to teach; you certainly have to be more patient than a lot of conductors.

Looking at the actual problem, we can't hope to have exciting poets, writers, composers and the rest in sufficient numbers who are in a sense "house trained" and can be turned loose in a high school in the next very short time. What I am suggesting is that many of those who are now in the teachers colleges have talent, more or less, and there are ways of teaching them to teach the arts. The way to do that is to put them with children, give them a chance to teach the arts to children because there is a wide-open field there. Nobody's doing it much, except in the nursery schools and only about eight percent of the kids of the country are in the nursery schools. Have student teachers go out and do street theater in Harlem, or in Huff in Cleveland, or whatever. Put them into situations where they learn to teach the arts with whatever talent they have as teachers or as artists and in that way develop a new attitude to what it means to teach the arts. I think there are many people who don't want to teach, who feel that by teaching they would inhibit their own creative work. And it is true, for some people it is impossible for them to start teaching without spoiling what they're really doing and what they feel is their own mission in life.

Comment. I wonder if what we are not saying is we are re-examining the art of teaching. I am reminded of Andrew Wyeth, who is a very verbal fellow about his art as artists go, and a very excellent teacher. He has an art style that I think we need. He is very communicative but not in terms of words and we as teachers tend to over-intellectualize, I believe. I think this is part of our publish or perish world which you have said, and I think quite rightly, is drawing up enthusiasm and creativity on our campus today, certainly killing curiosity—intellectual curiosity as well. I know an artist who teaches art who is a very disorganized fellow, who isn't quite sure of what he is going to do next and who could never possibly administer an art play, who has a sloppy art shop. But put students in his presence, give him a brush, let him put clay on their hands and magic occurs. This is the kind of communication that we need, and I think this is the emphasis we need in the art of teaching.

A. You say that beautifully. We'll quote you on that.

Comment. The teaching of music is likewise the art of unfolding and awakening the child's enthusiasm. Once the children get going they very often surpass the teacher.

THE DOMAINS OF KNOWLEDGE

GEORGE T. MATTHEWS

THE PURPOSE of this conference is to examine the role of the humanities in the curricula which we schoolmen devise for the torment of the young. In the previous conference the social sciences have been studied and the revolutionary impact of changes in the disciplines included in those categories of learning has been underscored. Over the years the public at large has been alerted to the exponential increase in knowledge in the natural sciences and the implication of this phenomenon upon high school and college programs of instruction. Equally important but less well known changes in the social sciences are beginning to reach the attention of literate audiences, and alterations in the curricula of these subjects have at least been suggested, even implemented in some places. It seems but just, therefore, that the third great division in the trinity of studies—the humanities—should now come up for discussion. Moreover, since the establishment of the National Foundation for the Arts and the Humanities in 1965, the prospect of federal largess to the humanities to match that so liberally advanced to the natural sciences since 1950 has added a sense of urgency to the enterprise. The idea of hundreds of millions of dollars flowing into humanistic activities frightens even as it whets the edge of academic appetite. No doubt, in the rush for financial nourishment, fear will be forgotten. It is then entirely appropriate that schoolmen should gather here and elsewhere to discuss the humanities and to contrive organizational and instructional techniques the better to reinforce, in our schools, the values of this third most ancient and most dignified of all the domains of knowledge.

In all that I have just said there is an assumption which I believe to be widely shared and accepted as valid: that the tripartite division of the categories of instruction and inquiry—the natural sciences, the social sciences, and the humanities—is not only logical and elegant, but neatly congruent with the reality and needs of education and research. So manifestly rational is this division of academic labor taken to be that it seems to have acquired the character of a natural law, to be as fixed and necessary as a constellation in the sky. C. P. Snow distinguished but two cultures—the humanistic and the scientific—in his famous lectures. In so far as esoteric curricula discussion has an effect beyond the conference hall, it would seem that there are three, not two, cultures in process of formation. In any event, as Professor John Higham of the University of Michigan has recently pointed out, the establishment of the National Foundation for the Arts and the Humanities may, ironically, deepen, through the power of money to create immutable bureaucratic distinctions, the schism in the academic soul which, contrary to some opinion, has shown impressive signs of healing along epistemological if not budgetary lines.

It is in light of these preliminary observations that I think it might be instructive to address myself to at least two aspects of our conference's major theme: first, what is meant by the term "the humanities," and how has that meaning come to be institutionaized in the universities of this country; and secondly, what seems to be meant by a humanistic approach to the experience of man and society.

I

The word "humanities" is of course very old. In English it seems first to have appeared in print in 1483, derived from the Italian form of the Latin *humanitatis*. In its original sense, the word referred to the education which was regarded as appropriate to a Roman gentleman, an education in intellectual and spiritual cultivation befitting a civilized member of the growing aristocracy of the late classical world. Such a humanistic education centered upon letters—the *literae humaniores*—and upon the possession and the exercise of the skills and sensibilities on which the practice of letters thrived. But this conception, at first sight narrow in spirit, was nourished by deep roots in Greek philosophy, particularly in that view which finds summary form in Aristotle's practical wisdom, that wisdom and the studies leading to it—politics, poetics, and ethics—which show a man how to live well. Thus the ancient humanities also embraced philosophy, including mathematics, and those matters

38

of direct concern to a member of the governing class: how first to rule himself that he might successfully rule others. A humanistic education was that which brought forth from the common clay of mankind those cultivated qualities on which the definition of humanity depended. Humanity was civilized mankind, and the chief vehicle of civilization was the humanities. Beyond humanity—civilized mankind—lay the barbarian, whether the external barbarian outside the Roman lines, or the internal barbarian of the lower classes. The concept of humanity was then normative and not descriptive. It rested upon a judgment as to the quality of a life and not only upon a record of overt behavior.

Ever since Roman times, the humanities—especial receptacle of the idea of humanity—have presented two aspects to the world. The one is ultimately mean in spirit. Restricted to a recondite exercise in remote languages, constricted to a niggardly identification of all civilized values to the values of a formal literature accessible only to a privileged few, the humanities as an educative mode often have been, and often still are, merely the reflection of the leisured taste and manners of a ruling elite. So narrowly confined to literary subjects narrowly interpreted and monopolized by gentlemen, the humanities served as a barrier against rather than as a way toward the wider diffusion of their own values. They were not civilized agencies, but instruments of spiritual exploitation. But on the other hand, the literature of the humanities possessed a great potential for enlargement of mind and spirit and for instruction in civic and ethical responsibility. The civilizing values they embodied were larger and more generous than the modish style of gentlemen. They formed a literature cultural base for the growth, not only of taste, but disciplined thought in an ample variety of human as well as humane concerns. They can be used to amplify and not to constrict the boundaries of humanity. These two aspects of the humanities have always been present, the one priggish, the other generous. One aspect or the other has tended to predominate in various times and places since the Antonines. The tension between the two has guaranteed to the idea of the humanities an astonishing endurance.

From Rome to Bloomfield Hills is a long road which mercifully I shall travel swiftly. During the Middle Ages the concept of *humanitatis* did not vanish, but letters were not the central preoccupation of the learned. The distinction that seemed important was not between civilization and barbarism, but between Christendom and the world of unbelievers, civilized or not. As to the rulers, the ethos of the war band, softened by the sentimentalities of Christian chivalry, sufficed.

For complex reasons I shall not go into here, the idea of the humanities reemerged in the first blush of that which, for want of a better term, we call the Renaissance. Humanism as an identifiable historical movement among the learned and literate classes of Europe spread from its center in Italy in the fifteenth and sixteenth centuries. Interested less in salvation than in temporal ethics, the humanist sought redemption in literature without denying the formal need for God's grace. Intent upon recapturing the spirit and knowledge as well as the eloquence of the ancients so long neglected—so the humanist thought—during the Gothic age that separated him from classical civilization, the humanist thrust Europe into a great age of erudition. Modern scholarship in spirit if not in form derives in large part from his initiative. Linguistics, philology, textural and literary criticism, etymology, diplomatics and history, comparative studies in religion and politics are but a sample of the list. The humanist, remote in time from the classical world he admired, invented the scholarly disciplines which could furnish a genuine knowledge of that world and make the antique tongues speak again. Moreover, being Christian, the humanist, certain of them at any rate, added Hebrew to the list of ancient languages and unlocked, to a far greater extent even than his Latin forebears, that Greek thought from which ultimately the philosophical aspects of the idea of the humanities derived. While the Latin classics ever remained the hearth, the house of humanistic interest was widened in the sixteenth and the seventeenth centuries to include new mansions. In the process the idea of humanity was extended to many diverse peoples and subjects. An appetite for a disciplined widening of human experience has been implicit in the humanities ever since.

But the humanist was more than a scholar. He was a schoolmaster. Convinced of the efficacy of literature as a civilizing agency, he sought to re-educate mankind by means of the ancient humanities refracted through the glass of Christian culture. Simultaneously the ruling aristocracies were hanging up their rusty armor in the cupboards of country manor houses as the rapidly changing world of the sixteenth and seventeenth centuries transformed them from feudal lords into officers and administrators, into courtiers and landed gentry. In a word, the governing classes once again comprised gentlemen; and the classical education revived by the humanists contained precisely that set of values which gentlemen needed in order to command authority in the society of the *ancien régime*. Humanist as schoolmaster and gentleman as pupil met in the classroom and forged, in the sixteenth century, the rudiments of that standard classical curriculum in the humanities—or as the University of Edinburgh rather grandly puts it, The Humanity— which dominated genteel education and set the style for all other forms of education down to the middle of the nineteenth century. To our ancestors of a hundred years ago the term "humanities" meant, to all intents and purposes, simply the study of Latin greats from Caesar to Cicero, with a little Greek for the very bright and a little Hebrew for the very pious. As that generous aspect of the revived humanities that appealed to the use of intellect and spirit in the confrontation of life was diffused into the general European culture, an important but often unrecognized component of the eighteenth-century Enlightenment, it lost identity. But that other aspect which appealed to class-bound snobbery prevailed in the formal systems of undergraduate education, particularly in England, homeland of the most secure aristocracy in the West.

Conceived simply as education for gentlemen and confined to a pedantic mastery of Latin prose, the humanities suffered severe limitations in the postrevolutionary, early industrial world of the nineteenth century. Confronted on the level of

41

intellectual relevance by the sheer brilliance and power of the emergent mathematical-empirical natural sciences, and by the transforming practicality of industrial technology on the level of social relevance, the classical humanities were driven to defend themselves in both the academy and the market place. Moreover, at the same time the dominance of gentlemen was challenged by the utility-minded middle classes, who more often than not spoke for the natural sciences and sought not only to include them in the curriculum but to displace the humanities from the educational enterprise.

The controversy, centering more in England than on the Continent, spilled over into the United States. But here the storm revolved around what was called the liberal arts, a broader, less defined term than the humanities, which in point of fact, used simply as a term, never enjoyed much currency in this country until the twentieth century. The term connoted classicism and class education to a degree unpalatable even to the East-coast Brahmins. A classical education was, in America as it was in England, the heart of collegiate education, but here classicism had been tempered and moderated by other, more pragmatic studies. Thus in the United States the issue was less between a narrowly defined classical curriculum and the natural sciences than between a liberally conceived education opposed to a technical or highly specialized education, no matter in what subject area. Moreover, the conflict was also institutional and involved the question of the place of the liberal arts college in the research-oriented universities that everywhere were abuilding in the post-Civil War era. In the United States the model of undergraduate education was the English residential college with its deep sense of community. But the model for graduate education was Continental, particularly German, with its emphasis upon the professionalization of the learned disciplines in all domains. In this tradition the controversy between the humanities and the natural sciences also was present, but the issues rarely concerned education *per se,* but rather the validity of each subject's claim to authentic knowledge and hence its claim to be recognized as a professional discipline. In the last third of the nineteenth century the American universities entered upon graduate research and became not only centers for the education of young men into proper styles of life, but centers for systematic discovery of new knowledge in all ranges of man's curiosity. The universities tended to overshadow the liberal arts colleges out of which many of them had grown. The fact that such colleges survived as viable vehicles for a liberally construed education depended in part upon a crucial redefinition of the humanities which was developed in England in the last half of the nineteenth century.

Although the intellectual ground of the natural sciences was itself one of the most significantly humane of all human accomplishments, science's champions in the nineteenth century trumpeted their claims to dominance in brash, even ungentlemanly ways. Nineteenth-century science was aggressively materialistic and mechanistic. Dependent upon elegant theoretical formulations of great speculative depth, the nineteenth-century scientist typically denied the role of speculation in the development of his ideas. He posed as a tough empiricist, even as his thought involved not only abstract mathematics, but imaginative leaps of great daring. Above all, his triumphs, which were undeniable, led him into pride. He proclaimed a monopoly on certain truth and attempted to engross all knowledge as his domain. With Karl Pierson, late nineteenth-century mechanistic science asserted that while it might be that scientists may never discover all that is worth knowing, all that is worth knowing can only be discovered by scientists.

The initial response of the defenders of the classical humanities was no less arrogant, even more shrill and lacking in candor. They fell back upon sheer piety and the worship of the established as the only good. In fact, the proponents of the classics were in the awkward position of defending the dominance of a social class, rather than the real worth of the humanistic tradition. But by the last half of the century that worth was rearticulated in terms that both preserved for the humanities their ancient sense of civilizing grace and adapted them to the new social situation of fluid class relations. It was discovered that the humanities, once extended beyond classicism, were admirably suited to the education of upward-mobile sons of the lower classes seeking, perhaps for the first time in history, to be full participants in the great tradition of civilized life. The humanities were redefined to become instruments of inclusion rather than instruments of exclusion for wider ranges of peoples into the high culture of the West. Literature continued to play a central role, although it functioned now as a window on the world rather than as an enchiridion of mental discipline. It was used to reveal the complexity of man's state and to convey moral, philosophical, even social ideas beyond those needed simply to train gentlemen. Moreover, the literatures of all humanity gradually took their seats among the Latins and the Greeks; in time, they reduced the classics to a minor place. But more significantly, the total meaning of the humanities was extended to embrace whatever subject dealt with man and his cultural activity. The idea of humanity was broadened to include all human acts. History, modern as well as ancient, philosophy, contemporary as well as Greek, politics, even economics, the comparative study of societies and religions were now admitted on equal plane with literature into the humanities curriculum. In scholarship the aim was systematic knowledge sought by whatever techniques were appropriate. In the universities the humanistic disciplines flourished, all tinctured with the historical and evolutionary bias that shaped nearly all scholarship of that time. On the Continent, in the United States, less so in England, humanistic scholarship was professionalized and pursued with an increasing bent toward specialization. But the educational function of the reformed humanities, oecumenically considered, was now generous and wide. It aimed, through a process of heightened self-consciousness achieved through the experience of literature, history, and philosophy, to break the mold of intellectual narrowness and social parochialism. It sought to provide a deep perspective on the present and to bring the student to a realization of his own potential as a civilized and humane man. In a word, from the chrysalis of a stuffy classicism the humanities emerged with the underlying philosophy of the modern concept of the liberal arts. Joined by

44

the sciences and mathematics, some of whose educational values were simultaneously redefined in the same liberal terms, the reformed humanities not only preserved their position but enlarged their influence in the total academic enterprise. The cost, however, should be noted: The classical humanities at least had a single, clearly defined subject matter—Latin and Greek literature. The reformed humanities contained such an array of disciplines that only statements of the most general sort could provide them with intellectual consistency.

By the end of the nineteenth century the war between the classical humanists and the natural scientists ended in a truce more or less amicably observed ever since. The youthful impudence of the scientists yielded to more mature attitudes. Fundamental renovations in the epistemological structure of the research by which the sciences proceeded, opened up a paradoxical vision. On the one hand the ability of science to probe deeper and deeper into the universe of nature seemed unlimitd; on the other, the sense of arriving at conclusive truths receded. The new physics of the twentieth century has a humility bred of great success. It recognizes the tentative nature of its own conclusions and the symbolic character of any set of truths. The possibility of many equally valid versions of reality was accepted by humanist and scientist alike. Meanwhile the reformed humanities had achieved an important redefinition of educational and scholarly function, while securing for literature important allies in disciplines hitherto uncommitted between the two camps. Thus two great domains of knowledge coexisted in the early twentieth century. By informal treaties that prevented pitched battles if not border raids, it was agreed that the domain of the natural sciences was to study nature, while that of the humanities was to study man in all his dimensions. In the universities neither was sovereign, but each was co-regent.

The divisions rested not so much upon a reasonable assignment of intellectual styles and methods as upon what appeared then to be a reasonable assignment of the subjects studied. In the domain of the sciences, inanimate and animate nature was the subject. In the domain of the humanities was the phenome-

45

non of man in all his dimensions: classics, languages, literature, philosophy, history, political science, anthropology, sociology and, by the end of the century, psychology. All of these and many more now comprised the humanities; indeed, in France they are still called *les sciences humaines*—the humane sciences, using the word "science" in its original sense of any body or systematic knowledge studied for its own sake. With this division of scholarly and educational labor the early twentieth century was sensibly content: the man-nature dualism seemed but common sense.

To the ear of the contemporary schoolman the list of subjects regarded as humanistic only sixty years ago seems odd, as much for its exclusions as for its inclusions. What we may call the creative arts are totally lacking. Painting, sculpture, music, the dance, theater, even the writing of poetry—all of the fine things that leap to mind when the word "humanities" is mentioned—then lay outside not only the humanistic domain but outside the academic realm altogether. The reformed humanities accepted the history, criticism and analysis of the arts as suitable subjects, but the act of engagement with paint, sound, stone, and bodily movement had no place. The cultivation of taste had of course always been a major function of the humanities, but humanists —save briefly in the Italian Renaissance—were never artists.

The reasons for this exclusion of the arts from the domain of the humanities are many, various, and highly complicated. But among them is the fact that the humanities, even after their reformation in the late nineteenth century, were and still are heavily literary and historical in character. The medium of their expression is normally words. Their method of analysis is the logical manipulation of verbal symbols, largely in linear narrative patterns. The humanities, more than the sciences, bear the mark of their descent from the Greeks, those passionate poets who sought to bridle passion with reason. The humanities deal with emotion-laden literature, with the human dimension of events, with matters requiring normative judgment. But the characteristic mode of their expression is abstract and generalizing, rather than phenomenological and concrete. Like all academic disciplines they are critical, analytical, and ultimately rationalistic.

But the creative arts are essentially non-linear in logic and existential in character. Further, since the late nineteenth century they have been militantly unhistorical and anti-literary in thrust. Modern movements in the arts—and they constitute one of the greatest creative moments in Western history—seem to seek to overthrow established forms, to push against the limits of existing paradigms in an effort to recast reality and test its limits. The creative arts of the twentieth century stem from a different level of the human intellect than academic rationality. It is a level that seeks reality subjectively, that seeks a personal ordering of experience, that fuses object and observer, that attempts to break down the barriers which the rational "I" puts between itself and experience. The creative arts represent a different dimension of humane reality than that easily conjured with in words, sentences, and narratives, the medium of the humanities for two thousand years. Thus for all presence of studios and concert halls on the campuses today, the academic humanist is still not fully convinced of the legitimacy of the creative arts' claim to admittance to his domain. One of the issues confronting the curriculum today is whether humanistic irony will be able to recognize the similarity between the present confrontation of the arts by the humanities and that older confrontation which involved the humanities with the natural sciences one hundred years ago. Surely it is not too much to hope that the humanity of the arts will be legitimized in good academic fashion. If not, the creative arts, which have already found allies in the creative sciences of nature, may carve out for themselves still another domain, if not of knowledge, then of experience.

If the exclusion of the creative arts from the accepted list of humanistic subjects in the early twentieth century piques the schoolman's interest, the inclusion of the range of subjects which we now call social sciences seems even more curious. Yet no less a person than John Dewey, in 1902, regarded history, sociology, political science, and political economy as humanistic subjects, despite their penchant, even then, for empirical methodology. It was the unexpected emergence of the social sciences, particularly in the United States, that upset the early twentieth-century scholastic equilibrium and divided all academe into three parts.

The dream of a positivistic, integrated science of man, modeled upon the methods of the natural sciences was, of course, of nineteenth-century origin. Indeed political economy, the oldest, most rationalistic of the social sciences, antedates the nineteenth century, while political science, sociology, and anthropology were established as separate disciplines about the middle of the century. At about the same time psychology broke away from its parent philosophy and achieved status as a separate discipline toward the end of the century. But these infant disciplines, still too young to enter the lists in the war between the natural scientists and the humanists, developed virtually no collective cohesion before the twentieth century. While they attempted to employ the empirical methods of the natural sciences, their subject matter was clearly man and his works. Moreover, most were imbued with the evolutionary-historical schema that dominated the intellectual life of the times and so were indebted to, indeed were often indistinguishable from, history, then in its majestic prime. As I have pointed out, in Europe the social sciences even today are not regarded as a distinct group of disciplines with distinct subject matter and methods, although American influence since World War II is beginning to effect changes.

The social sciences first achieved academic identity in the United States. But even here the situation was fluid through the First World War to the establishment of the American Council of Learned Societies in 1919. That body, now considered a citadel of the humanities, originally contained all the professional organizations representing the social sciences, as well as those concerned with the humanities. But in the nineteen-twenties certain young scholars, who identified themselves with the social sciences, began aggressively to establish their claim to independent status and to pull away from the older

48

cultural studies. The success in applying statistical methods developed in the natural sciences to the study of man and society placed in their hands tools of great analytical power which was only amplified by the advent of the computers in the nineteen-fifties. Attracted by the prestige enjoyed by science in America, the young social scientists—they insisted on the phrase—forged a professional identity which consciously excluded the students of literature, art, and philosophy. They differed from the scholars of the older cultural subjects not only in method but in avowed aim. The intent of the generation of social scientists bred in the nineteen-twenties—those who dominated the graduate departments in the thirties and forties and who trained the social scientists of today—was to create a pure science of human behavior, free of humanistic speculation and void of normative considerations. In this science value judgements—the phrase was first heard at this time—were to be eliminated from the process of inquiry and man would be accepted as he is. The model was physics, not literature; the subject was man, not nature; but it was also not man in the sense of humanity. That was a value freighted term left to the humanists to waste their time with. In 1923 the Social Science Research Council broke away from the American Council of Learned Societies. In 1928 the Rockefeller Foundation recognized the intellectual revolution that was taking place and formed a Division of Social Sciences separate from the Division of Humanities (the two have recently been joined again, perhaps a sign of the future). The universities followed suit and by the end of the Second World War it was clear that in the United States three, not two, academic domains of knowledge were in existence. The queens of the humanities might join the kings of the natural sciences at faculty clubs in a bit of amused raillery at the expense of the academic parvenues—they were especially scornful of the uncivilized language of the newcomers—but it was evident that the study of man was no longer the monopoly of any one set of disciplines. This became especially clear when, in 1950, the National Science Foundation, that source of power and prestige, proceeded to support those social sciences which "can be studied by objective methods which will yield verifiable results." There has been money in the behavioral sciences ever since. As if to consummate the growing bifurcation of man as a subject of academic concern, which to some degree the development of the social sciences as an academic domain has entailed, the newly established National Endowment for the Humanities has defined the humanities as literature, linguistics, history, philosophy, archaeology, jurisprudence, the study of art and music, and "those aspects of the social sciences which have humanistic content and employ humanistic methods." Whether this reference to the humanistic aspects of the social sciences was intended as irony I do not know, but it points to an era of confusion in academic organization, especially if the National Foundation for the Arts and the Humanities ever really receives funding on a par with the National Science Foundation. For who is to say when a method is humanistic rather than objective, and what are the criteria of verifiable results?

II

Is there a core of disciplines which according to the prevailing practices of university administration and scholarly agreement may be identified as within the domain of the humanities? The answer is affirmative if literature, the study of languages as part of the study of literature, philosophy, the history of art, the theoretical and scholarly aspects of the study of music, are all that is meant. But history is regarded as much a social science as a part of the humanities, if the practices of different universities are surveyed; linguistics is or is not a part of the humanities, depending upon local accident. As to the practice or the performance of art and music, only rarely are these arts included in the humanistic domain. On university campuses there is most often a complete lack of communication between the artists and the scholars, often to the mutual satisfaction of both parties. Further, while literature, history, and philosophy (or at least the more old-fashioned elements of that mother of wisdom) have much in common, music, aside from scholarship in music history, is often pursued in isolation of the rest. In a word, there is little internal consistency in the domain of the humanities. Among the social sciences there is a similar undeviant core of disciplines, with others added or subtracted according to local circumstances. Anthropology, sociology, and political science are the core of the social sciences. But it is not infrequent to find economics within the sciences, while psychology, like history a genuine swing discipline, is as often a part of the domain of natural science as it is of social science, again depending upon the local situation and traditions. I will not go into the situation in regard to the natural sciences, except to point out that mathematics, while most commonly found in the domain of the natural sciences, is sometimes found in the humanities—a practice consistent with ancient tradition running back some two thousand years. Yet mathematics, one of the most humane of human activities, rarely ever is considered today as a part of *humanitatis*, much to the chagrin of many mathematicians, I should add.

With this brief outline of common academic administrative practice in mind, let me examine briefly the degree to which we may ascribe common intellectual traits in subject matter, methods of inquiry, modes of approach to experience to each of the three major groupings of academic disciplines. It is evident that the humanities, by custom and common agreement, possess a core of disciplines which are linguistical and literary in tone; it is also evident that the humanities contain an additional clientage which can be given a sense of cohesion, either from the point of view of methods or of subject, only by a considerable exercise of rhetoric. The ease and speed with which the social sciences—the subject matter of which were, only fifty years ago, considered as humanistic—have established both in academic and in popular consciousness a separate professional identity, demonstrates the point, at least in this country. The humanities can no longer claim a distinctive subject matter, the study of man and his cultural experience. However, a similar statement can be made about the social sciences. The integrated science of man, dreamt of by the young Turks of the nineteen-twenties, has not yet emerged, although there is still a thrust in that direction, one which has been building up momentum once again in recent years. But that thrust is now highly sophisticated, and with the kind of assurance bred of success seems likely to repeat the earlier pattern of the natural sciences. Tolerance of other methods, recognition that normative concerns and personal judgments can never be totally excluded from the study of man, has not slackened the drive of certain practitioners in the social sciences to approximate the methods of the natural sciences, but it has moderated their earlier scorn of alternative approaches.

Is there a characteristic method, approach, or style which is uniquely humanistic or uniquely scientific in regard to man and society? The recent attempts to articulate a curriculum according to underlying structures of knowledge have failed to reveal such a rigid distinction. Rather, a continuous spectrum seems to exist, with gross distinctions possible between the extremes only. By science we commonly mean the logical ordering of knowledge into general laws that can be publicly verified and which contain a high degree of predictability. Science tends to progress—it might be argued that scientific knowledge is the only kind of knowledge that can be called progressive, implying no connotation of better or worse to that word—on the basis of what has been called its detachable conclusions. That is, once a conclusion has been established—verified and proven by whatever canons are deemed sufficient—the process of verification need not be repeated, and the conclusion joins the firm foundation from which the next step is made. Science proceeds logically from one conclusion to another. Further, science is analytical in nature and relies upon rigorous definition of concepts of wide generality. Such concepts are most often based upon empirical evidence and are most often stated in mathematical terms. Science tends to be quantitative and experimental, but these latter are not indispenable. Carefully organized observation combined with logical inference may take the place of experimentation. Thus the astronomer cannot experiment with the stars any more than can the historian with history. Yet neither is simply a passive camera of observation: each uses conceptual structures to tell him what to look for; each uses judgment to assess what he has seen. Speculation and imagination are by no means absent in the sciences, but the results of such exercises must in the end be publicly verifiable, that is, the conclusions arrived at must be capable of being demonstrated again by any person, at any time, and in any place. Most commonly associated with the natural sciences, these characteristics of scientific procedure are not preempted by them. In the study of human acts and activities, such procedures are fruitful to different degrees and with different sorts of information. Thus econometrics, which attempts to study the operation of that eminently human system, the economy, finds itself quite capable of generating general laws with a fairly high level of predictability based upon data derived empirically and analyzed statistically. Thus experimental psychology, which seeks to determine regularities of behavior using experimental systems, is remarkably close to physiology in method and aim.

The methods most commonly associated with a humanistic approach are actually to be found as ingredients in all branches of scholarship, certainly in large areas of the social sciences and even in some areas of the natural sciences, such as historical geology and taxonomic biology. Does the classification of biological genera differ in any significant methodological manner from the classification of pottery series unearthed at an archaeological dig? But in contrast to what we may call scientific methodology, that connected with humanistic study displays much less coherence and much greater diversity. There is no one single strategy of scholarship that can be identified as humanistic in any precise fashion. As John Higham suggests, "Perhaps the most that can be said is that humanistic approaches predominate in all efforts to preserve complexity of experience instead of abstracting verifiable regularities from it." Thus the historian as humanist may be keenly aware of the accidental or contingent in human events, may insist upon the unique personality and its bearing upon the course of events, and may be concerned with particularity rather than generality. But the historian as social scientist may be concerned with the origin and development of political, social, or economic systems or the relation of ideas to cultural institutions. He is no less a historian than his humanist colleague; indeed, he may be the same man seeking different answers to different questions at different times in his attempt to understand the past. The historian as humanist may be concerned with a unique event, and use all the resources of statistical analysis to measure that event. The historian as social scientist may be seeking the general patterns or configurations of historical movement and employ a high degree of intuition—rapid leaps of synthesizing intelligence—in his quest. Again it may be the same historian working on two different levels of generality and employing methods appropriate to each. Is he social scientist or humanist? Nevertheless, it is true that the humanities as a group tend to have a broader tolerance for intuitively derived statements and a narrower tolerance for the need of public verification than the social sciences. Thus in the extreme, humanistic scholarship has but few detachable conclusions. The critical judgment of the student of literature cannot depend simply upon reading what other critics have said about an author's work; the author's work must be read and read again by successive generations of critics; and no final conclusion will be reached, as the movement in and out of critical acclaim of nearly all writers of the past will attest. Such procedure is not progressive in the scientific sense of the word; but it is not regressive either, for the attempt here is not so much the accumulation of authenticated knowledge as the perpetual testing of responses among human beings. By like token, the same critic may act as editor of a critical edition of an author's works and so produce volumes of scholarship which will never be contested.

In the humanities there is a greater reliance upon the use of verbal as opposed to non-verbal systems or symbolization. There is a greater acceptance of qualitative language as opposed to quantitative expression. There is a greater degree of willingness to accept normative judgment as integral to the humanistic approach; but exceptions abound, and the true scholar in the humanities is as concerned with approximating reality in his statements as the sociologist or the physicist, while the social scientist is aware of the need for evaluative statements and, nowadays, rarely hesitates to make them when need arises. The humanistic scholar examines his assumptions no less rigorously than the social scientist, and both owe an equal debt of candor to their publics. But neither is exempt from the critical appraisal of peers, which each accepts gratefully or at least with good public grace if he is playing faithful to his role as scholar. Perhaps, in conclusion, it may be said that humanistic learning depends to a greater degree than scientific learning upon the maturity of the scholar as a man, for he typically deals with human products the ramifications of which often can be fully understood only through the experience of life itself.

I have just recounted what may be thought of as the chief characteristic of humanistic method or approach. But even in total they could not be said to constitute a single, organized, distinctive method, as I have tried to show as I went along. It is a matter of more or less. If one attempts to force any segment of the spectrum of approaches or methods that ranges from the humanistic to the scientific at the extremes to correspond with any one of the major domains of knowledge, or certainly with any one of the numerous disciplines each is thought to comprise, the effort proves fruitless.

In truth it is very difficult to make distinctions even in gross, for there is a great interchange of methods going on. A single student of literature may at the same time be engaged in historical criticism, deeply involved in an analysis of the effects of non-literary elements upon literature (for example, psychological or sociological elements for other purposes), and be running a word count or item analysis through the computer, using the most sophisticated techniques deriving from matrix algebra. As another example, at the institution of which I am a member, a young scholar of great sensitivity whose main area of interest is ancient Chinese philosophy, is engaged in research on Chinese semantics that keeps him in the Computer Data Processing Center more hours than in the library. Another scholar, an expert on the poet W. H. Auden, is heavily involved with an econometrician in the development of a learning model based upon information-retrieval theory. Both these scholars regard themselves as humanists, each is currently engaged in research the methods of which are drawn directly from the social sciences. Admittedly these are unusual men, but they are not unique.

Perhaps humanistic studies may be distinguished from scientific studies less by method—the procedures and canons of inquiry—than by those aspects of human experience they choose to study. It cannot be gainsaid that the student of literature chooses to study a human product—literature—while the student of anthropology chooses to study a kinship system—an equally human product. While literature and kinship systems are both products of the activity of man, they may elicit different responses to different sorts of questions. There are, of course, some rough distinctions that can be made along these lines. The humanist generally is interested in the discrete products of man—his art, his literature, his music—while the social scientist is more interested professionally in the abstract systems of society which sustain or inhibit the production of art, literature, or music. All this is true enough, but only by and large. Each approach shades imperceptibly into the other, and no absolute discrimination can be finally made within this gambit.

The argument may be made that only the humanist is concerned as a scholar, with the humane as contrasted to the merely human, that he is the keeper of the ancient concept of *humanitatis*, the concept that insists that while anything a man can do may be called human, not everything he does deserves to be called humane. That humanists often claim to be exclusively concerned with the kinds of human acts that reveal man as humane is quite true. That humanists often regard themselves as the guardians of a treasured humane heritage of freedom and spirit is also true; indeed, some humanists never let you forget it. But the quality of humaneness is surely not the privileged possession of any group of scholars. Is it any more humane to study a work of art than a theory in physics? Or is either art or physics less a humane product than the other? Does either express the spirit of man more radically than the

56

other? I do not believe so. Yet it is the humanist who studies art, and the physicist who studies physics. Neither can claim advantage over the other in concern for the humanity of man. The idea of *humanitatis,* once the possession of a narrow segment of humanity, has now been placed within the reach of nearly all. We owe a debt to those old humanists who, through education, preserved and nourished the idea of humanity. Perhaps we even owe a debt to those gentlemen who, often for wrong reasons but sometimes for right ones, made it possible for the concept to survive. Perhaps we owe a debt to ourselves to make the concept of humanity more of a reality to as many as possible within a world which is, not unexpectedly, quite inhumane.

▲   ▲   ▲

THE MUSEUM IN THE HUMANITIES

FREDERICK L. RATH, JR.

IT WAS with considerable awe that I listened to Dr. Taylor's fine talk this morning. More than awe, perhaps; for he knows what he is talking about—obviously. I have the feeling that what I must do—possibly uncharacteristically—is to "put on the napless vestment of humility." For my topic, as you know, is "The Museum in the Humanities"—and, after a month of mental struggle, I'm not certain what it means or what I can do with it.

Under the circumstances the only decent thing I *can* do is to enter on the record the disclaimer offered by the great 19th century humorist, Artemus Ward, who was wont to open his talks with the forthright statement: "The principal feature of my lecture is that it contains so many things that have nothing to do with it."

Not really, of course! But I would make it clear that I am *not* an educator in the sense that you are educators. What I know about educational theory and practice was not derived from classroom lectures. I am an historian who, by an accident of fate, wandered into the field of historic preservation exactly thirty years ago and has been wrestling ever since with some elusive ideas in what I am going to call roadside education. What I chose to be called is an interpreter—a term I shall define later. If I succeed in making you understand interpretation as we use the term in museums, then you may understand a little better the role played by some of the humanities in some of the museums.

Note my caution—"the role played by some of the humanities in some of the museums." I want to define the boundaries so that I stay clearly within the limits of my own experience. To do so, let me note that Dr. Henry Allen Moe, Chairman of the Board of our New York State Historical Association, served a brief term as first Chairman of the new National Endowment for the Humanities and coined the term "humanistic museums." It is a portmanteau phrase to embrace those museums that are not art museums or science museums. He included museums of history, archaeology, and anthropology, as well as historic sites, buildings; and, as he said, "perhaps more," confessing that at this moment of our development, we simply don't know.

The reason for this seemingly ignorance or obtuseness may not be clearly apparent to you. It is bound up with the startling growth of the museum movement itself, especially in the last forty years. As a direct result of 20th century forces such as the rise of mass culture, about which Dr. Taylor talked so brilliantly; the rising educational level in our schools, colleges, and universities; shorter work weeks with increased leisure time; longer paid vacations and the increased pay that have made travel possible; and the greater number of automobiles traveling billions of miles annually on the new parkways, throughways, and turnpikes; our humanistic museums are dealing with what I believe to be the largest audience ever attracted to any branch of education. It has been estimated that last year, for example, more than 100,000,000 visits were made to the humanistic museums with which I am dealing here. That the result of this influx has not been utter chaos is, perhaps, a testimonial to the calibre of the men and women who have come to work for these museums.

What I am more concerned with now, however, are the implications of this development. You will remember that the concept of the museum as a temple of the Muses is itself rooted in antiquity. But until relatively recently museums were viewed primarily as repositories for the use of a small intellectually elite class. Although the seeds of change were being sown by the middle of the 19th century, it is only within the lifetimes of many of us here today that those seeds began to blossom and bear fruit. And if sometimes you detect groping and uncertainty among those of us attached to this new profession, you will appreciate that some of the flowering was strange fruit. First we had to become accustomed to dealing with a tidal wave of museums *viewers,* the hosts of the curious newly involved in what might be called "elective education." It imposed strains for which we were ill prepared. No longer could we be solely institutions designed for the collection of materials and objects

60

with sidelines of genealogy and research and of desultory display. Gradually it was borne in upon us that we had to become educational institutions with well-rounded programs and a mission to use our materials for the benefit of our fellows. For the sake of these museum viewers we had to sharpen our practices. To some degree at least we had to re-direct our research, away from the pedantic and esoteric to what I am going to call with some hesitancy a more popular scholarship, albeit just as sound and perhaps even a bit more scientific. We had to learn how to present our materials so that we could capture the attention and the interests of a seemingly endless chain of non-captive audiences. We had to learn how to conserve our materials in the light of the new pressures and the new forces. We had to try to stem the forces destroying the materials and objects, including historic sites and buildings, which were deemed significant by nationally recognized criteria.

Until very recently then we were concerned primarily with the problems posed by museum viewers—and as I now virtually abandon that subject I do not want to suggest for a moment that we have solved all of those problems. We have not. But we are working on them and they interlock with the subject of this conference: the exploration of and planning for humanities teaching in the elementary and secondary schools.

Now, in what is deliberate oversimplification, in contradistinction to the term I have been using, "museum viewers," let me introduce the term "museum *users*." Today there are many categories of museum users and I shall make no attempt to speak for all of them, for they represent problems to which we are also trying to give attention. What you and I are concerned with here, however, is the teacher and the student at the elementary and secondary school level and their use of the humanistic museums and their materials. There is not time enough to stray from the point.

During the last 35 years and most notably since the end of World War II, ever greater numbers of school children have been brought to museums in groups. To meet this often overwhelming surge, the museums of this country have tried to strengthen their staffs and their educational programs, sometimes successfully. What is now apparent, I think, is that only a part of the job can be done in the museums themselves, no matter how well and carefully museums and schools cooperate. There simply are physical limitations and logistical problems that cannot be overcome. For example, in Cooperstown, our Farmers' Museum, which is administered by the New York State Historical Association, in a seven-week period last year between May 1, when the museum is activated with full staff, and mid-June when the schools closed, dealt with 20,000 school children in groups. It was, I think, generally well done by a corps of specially trained housewife-guides in groups of 30 or less. All teachers had received a kit of educational materials and were given the opportunity to indicate where they wanted stress to be laid in the presentation so that it might fit in with their curriculum needs. During recent years most of our strong museums have been able to develop programs of this sort, and I would say in general that teachers are satisfied with the results. But the point—at least for us—is that we have reached our peak. There is literally no way that we can shoehorn more groups through The Farmers' Museum between the hours of ten and two in this seven-week period. And all of our efforts to have teachers schedule these trips at other times of the year have been to no avail. Even now, because we work with some pride, we are concerned. And it is this concern which has led to some further thinking and to some experiments that may interest you and may point to a somewhat different role for humanistic museums in the future.

The late Ernest Martin Hopkins, onetime president of Dartmouth College, in his oral reminiscences, has told how a former president talked him into serious consideration of the presidency by saying to him, "You're a gambler" and "Dartmouth's at the stage where it needs gambling [in its educational program]." Reflecting on this later in life, Hopkins concluded: ". . . educational progress *is* a gamble. I think you've got to gamble."

As I see it, the gamble in education lies in our willingness to experiment. I remember with the greatest pleasure the attitude of the man who befriended our New York State Historical Association and made possible the program which we undertake there, the late Stephen C. Clark. Always when we laid before him a well-conceived new project he would say, "Why don't we try it? How will we know unless we try it?" The true greatness of the response lay in the fact that he accepted the possibility of failure. He recognized that to a degree at least we were—or should be—kin to the physicist or the chemist in his laboratory. He trusted us to learn from our failures, possibly even to find the right path *because of* our failures. Or, to express it another way, he who has never been lost has almost certainly never been found.

Now I want to cast back some eight or nine years to a summer evening in Cooperstown when I found myself discussing the social studies programs in the elementary and secondary schools in our state with a dynamic and bright woman named Hazel Hertzberg. She was one of our Yorker sponsors—and I should say that our Association has 10,000 junior members called Yorkers and banded together into history clubs in some 250 schools throughout the state. The story of this development since 1942 might be enlarged upon as another aspect of the teaching of the humanities in museums and schools, but it is not the major point today. Mrs. Hertzberg was also a teacher of 7th grade social studies who had come to know our museums and our resources well. Excitedly, we were exchanging ideas and points of view; significantly, most of it stemmed from dissatisfaction. She wasn't happy about what was happening in the teaching of social studies in the schools and I wasn't happy about the role of the museums. Suddenly, we found ourselves agreeing that what we really needed in all elementary and secondary schools was history laboratories and workshops similar to our physics laboratories, our chemistry laboratories, and our biology laboratories.

In the years that ensued, we began slowly to develop some ideas. We began to take note of others, like Dr. John Anthony Scott of Fieldstone School, Riverdale, New York, who was reaching in the same direction but from a different angle. Mrs. Hertzberg herself began to strengthen the concept, the methods, and the techniques in her own classroom. We tried, haltingly and sometimes ineffectually, I admit, to expand the ideas and in a sense to test them.

The break came in 1964 when two separate curriculum-study committees in our State Department of Education suggested that the study of state and local history at the seventh grade level, mandated in New York since 1942, be abandoned in favor of the study of Latin American and Canadian history. The New York State Historical Association—which, by the way, despite its name, is not State-supported, but is an independent, private, nonprofit educational institution chartered by the Board of Regents—blew its collective top. I need hardly point out that we believe in state and local history and I am not going to spend time this morning to adduce our arguments in its favor. I must point out, however, that our point of view prevailed and the recommended changes were not effectuated.

But we felt, rightly, that some additional burden was now on us. By this time, fortunately, we were in a stronger position and we had on our staff a former social studies teacher and Yorker sponsor, Milo V. Stewart, as head of our very small education department. Far better than Dr. Louis C. Jones, our Director, or I, he knew the school system, and he was quick to grasp the concepts of new uses for the materials of the past and to suggest how they might be used in the classroom. Moreover, Mrs. Hertzberg by this time had a new affiliation with Teachers College, Columbia University, where she was teaching and continuing her work for a doctor of philosophy degree.

Condensing a long story drastically, it came about that Mrs. Hertzberg was invited by the State Education Department to help to revise the seventh grade social studies curriculum. Although what she started (the revision is not yet complete) is important, what is even more significant is what is emanating from that revision, and I want to deal with that first. As Mrs. Hertzberg and others worked on the first unit to be published,

"Teaching the Age of Homespun," she and Mr. Stewart realized that there was a serious flaw in the project. So many new ideas, new approaches, and new techniques were being introduced that it would be necessary to teach the teachers how to teach it, as was already being done in math and science. And so in the summer of 1965 the New York State Historical Association and the State University College at Oneonta, with a grant from the Bureau of Teacher Education of the State Education Department, offered to twenty carefully selected social-studies teachers and supervisors what was called Summer Seminar on Seventh Grade Social Studies, using the Association's museums as laboratory, workshop, and classroom, and centered on the Age of Homespun.

The importance of what was to be offered that summer was evident in the statement of the major aims of the three-week course: to increase the teacher's knowledge of selected areas of New York State's culture; to introduce teachers to the use of an interdisciplinary approach and discovery method in the teaching of 7th grade social studies; and to acquaint teachers with appropriate instructional materials for 7th grade social studies, with emphasis on the use of primary sources. Just as significant was a re-seeding idea that was built into the offering, which had been introduced into the math and science teaching projects. To teach some 20 teachers was like trying to create a forest from only 20 seeds. Perhaps it was from this very analogy that sprang the idea of re-seeding. In any event, no applicant was acceptable until the cooperating school or school district indicated its williingness to conduct a regional social studies center for teachers during the following school year, to be taught by the applicant. Furthermore, each of these instructors receives a salary of $640 for conducting these regional programs, half of which must be paid by the cooperating school or school district.

Let me jump ahead now just a bit and say that the Social Studies Seminar succeeded so well in 1965 that during the next summer the presentation was expanded, in fact doubled. This was possible because a new unit on the Pre-Columbian Iroquois, the author of which was again Mrs. Hertzberg, had been published by the State Department of Education. Much of the material for this publication was developed through the Anthropology Curriculum Study Project of the American Anthropological Association, one of the first and best of the new social studies curriculum projects. Thus, the two units to be taught in the 1966 Seminar represented a unique collaboration among an historical association and its museums, a curriculum project sponsored by a learned society, a State Department of Education, a college (Oneonta) in the State University of New York, and classroom teachers.

As a result of this collaboration, 38 teachers and supervisors of social studies came to us last August and all (or almost all) now have set up their own regional studies centers throughout New York State. Right now there are 575 social studies teachers attending these re-seeding courses. They are learning that history, archaeology, and other humanistic disciplines can be brought to bear upon significant topics in each cultural period. In both the Homespun and Iroquois studies they are learning to deal in depth with such cultural topics as patterns of space, patterns of time, the family, the life cycle, agriculture, the roles of men and women, non-farming activities, and the functions of the economy. They are considering the cultural aspects unique and common to each of these periods. They are receiving kits of special teaching materials (filmstrips, books, pamphlets, tapes, visuals), largely derived from the resources of our own museums. (In addition to The Farmers' Museum, an outdoor folk museum covering the period from 1783 to 1860, we administer Fenimore House, which features a superb collection of American Folk Art.) They are also learning to seek out in their own communities and neighborhoods the artifacts that illuminate the past. What is more, although they are largely people of the book, they are learning to read the artifact. Only rarely in the past has the scholar used the three-dimensional materials that comprise the holdings of the humanistic museums; even more rarely does the teacher know how to use and to interpret them.

What we are trying to do, then, is to combine our strengths.

Earlier I called myself, proudly, an interpreter, and the time has come to define interpretation. It is, I think, inspired revelation, based on sound scientific scholarship and designed to make people think for themselves about meanings and ideas and relationships in the past. In dealing with *our* noncaptive audiences we in the museum field have been forced to learn that they can and will walk out on us and not return unless we can attract as well as instruct, unless we can help them to see by skillful use and interpretation of our materials. We must select our materials carefully (for, in truth, we have so much); we must present them lucidly and graphically; we must synthesize them artfully; we must have the intelligence to display them so that the capacity of our viewers and users will be stimulated and even taxed. We believe that out of the complexities, ambiguities, and paradoxes of human history can come comprehensive simplicities. We even believe in the sounds, smells, and feel of the past: the rhythmic chunk of a churn, the clank of a lid on a Dutch oven; herbs drying, spicy pomanders, homemade soap; the silkiness of flax, the patina and balanced perfection of a hay fork carved from the forest a century and a half ago, the roughness of linsey-woolsey, the smoothness of a musket barrel. All these—and more—are transferrable to the classroom, or, better, to the history workshop and laboratory. Is it not wiser to try to capture the spirit of the past rather than the so-elusive past itself? And it is not possible to re-create the spirit of the past through the imaginative and ingenious use of our heritage? Can we not let our historical scholarship crystallize as understanding if we deal in human and truthful terms with a past that was real? If it is education that gives the common man a background for being a responsible member of his society, it is interpretation—the inspired revelation designed to make man think for himself—that produces the uncommon man, the leader.

Perhaps, then, this is what the humanistic museums can offer to you—a new approach to the social studies. For this is our strength—or should be. We have been termed "the unintegrated step-children of our educational enterprise" and we deserve the label in many instances. But I submit that with your cooperation and your understanding the gap can be bridged, and you will profit and so shall we.

For there are, I think, some national trends in the social studies which can be identified and which may be useful to us in further defining our hopes for the future. Having received very considerable help from Mrs. Hertzberg, let me try to enumerate some of them.

The wave of innovation and change in curriculum, which started in mathematics and the sciences, has been spreading rapidly in recent years to other subjects, including the social studies. Much of the initiative for curriculum reform, I have been told, came largely from outside the field of professional education and was led by university people. But it has been realized by us that the critical problem was to mix together competence in both subject matter and pedagogy, at the same time stirring in a new ingredient, the human and material resources of our museums. To do this, it was our view that the classroom teacher was central to the educational process and that only with his or her help could there be a successful creation of new materials and an imaginative and educationally useful approach to old materials.

Also noted as a national trend was the creation and development of materials designed for particular courses and even for particular units in courses, not only for students but also for teachers. The result of this "package conception" in the instance I am citing is illustrated by two manuals, "Teaching Pre-Columbian Culture: the Iroquois" and "Teaching the Age of Homespun." The units are chronologically arranged and go from the relatively simple to the more complex. The effect is intended to be cumulative, so that the student gradually acquires a number of perspectives and analytical tools to use in subsequent units, so that he may make significant cross-cultural comparisons, and so that each unit sheds further light on the one already studied. These units do not include detailed lesson plans. They are designed to provide a firm structure within which a good deal of flexibility is possible, depending on teacher strengths, student ability levels, socio-economic factors, and the location of the schools. Although we recognize that *how* learning takes place is still a moot question, we know that students should be taught so as to build on their strengths at their particular levels of development, and these units were created to do this.

What is more, these guides evidence recognition of another national trend in the use of an interdisciplinary approach, stressing central concepts and methodologies of the disciplines concerned. Both units have an historical perspective, but "Homespun" deals specifically with training in historical method, while the "Pre-Columbian Culture" leans heavily on anthropology. (In passing, let me remark that of eight units in the new syllabus four using the interdisciplinary approach are planned and the guide for "The Emerging City," with its primary emphasis on migration, will employ sociology as its central discipline, while the guide for "The Contemporary City" will center around urban geography.)

We have noted yet another national trend among educators: the use of the discovery method and of inductive teaching and the resultant need for specific materials designed to enable the discovery to take place. And here, of course, is our strength: museums and historical societies are depositories for the primary materials of the past. What teachers must learn is how to use these materials—and their trained interpreters; what we must learn, in addition to the nature of your classroom problems, is to make our human and material resources more readily available either in direct or indirect ways. Toward this end we are conducting many experiments ranging from the very simple to the complex. For example, the development of custom-made educational materials on the Age of Homespun, the Iroquois, and the City, such as sound film strips, sound tapes and records, reproduction of primary materials on mimeograph sheets, and even telephonic hook-ups with classrooms, with our own experts interpreting our materials as they appear in coordinated slide shows. In an electronic age the possibilities, as we see it, are almost infinite. What is significant here, of course, is the role that one humanistic agency with several museums under its

69

wing is trying to do: to assist in the development and dissemination of human and material resources. Since most commercial companies tend not to deal with so small a market (specific units in one grade in one state), it was necessary for us to try to fill the gap. This has become a pioneering mission.

Let me also point out that we had noted, of course, that the trend in social studies is toward in-depth studies in place of surveys. A course in state and local history, limited in both time and space, seemed to be one of the best places to use the in-depth approach. We wanted to show how, on the same geographical stage, a number of varying cultures could flourish and how a number of different kinds of responses to it could and did take place; how different people at different times perceived and used the same geographical setting and natural resources; how one can look in depth into one's own community past and discover patterns as well as unique qualities. We believe that by studying the familiar, students can better understand the unfamiliar. Thus, tribal cultures in the world today may be more readily understood if the Iroquois culture has been explored; today's rural societies are better understood if the Age of Homespun has been studied; the functioning and increasing dominance of the city as a world-wide phenomenon will be better understood if pupils have studied the growth and functioning of their own cities. We also feel that the new approach can give urban children perspective on the rural past and rural children perspective on the city.

Where then do we stand today? You, charged with the great responsibility of educating our young, are seeking new and better ways to fulfill your mission. We, the collectors, conservators, and interpreters of this nation's heritage, lacking your own long history as educational professionals, are seeking ways to assist. To me, it does not seem that friendly cooperation is an impossible proposition if we each have respect for and understanding of the other. There is much, especially in the humanities, that we can do well together that we shall do less well separately. Perhaps we should remind ourselves that the first requirement of the humanities is that they be humane—that is, human and not pendantic. And lest you think that this is a stricture leveled only against you, let me tell you that I remember with a wince that it was a member of *my* profession who once defined historic houses as "large habitat groups of human material." We too have some brush to clear. We might also remind ourselves that Henry Adams once noted that "Unless education marches on both feet—theory and practice—it risks going astray . . . " It is necessary for us to theorize and to practice—and to experiment and even gamble—together for the common good.

I think that we in the humanistic museums are readying ourselves for that challenge, for I would remind you that while of necessity I have talked almost exclusively of one phase of the work that we are doing at the New York State Historical Association, there are others who are also thinking long thoughts about our role and mission. I noticed just the other day, for example, that in Fort Worth, Texas, a new Museums Resources Council has been created, to develop new and broader uses of educational resources and it was stated, "We hope that these resources may become a vital component in the public education system, and through adult education programs, to the general public." Old Sturbridge Village, with a small grant from a foundation and in cooperation with the School of Education, University of Massachusetts, is planning two teacher workshops at the Village this winter and spring to provide first-hand experience in the use of its resources in the teaching of American history. The Whitney Museum of American Art (New York City), in cooperation with the Smithsonian Institution, has just announced a project to explore the feasibility of branch museums; the same fund will underwrite a six-week summer institute for public school teachers, to acquaint them with new art techniques and media and some aspects of science. Title III of the Elementary and Secondary Education Act of 1965 is making available money for resource surveys and for the establishment of instructional resource centers throughout the country, centers which are designed to make more effective use of cultural agencies and cultural resources. And in a few places, such as Amsterdam, New York, inspired educators are weaving into the fabric of their own school programs the preservation of buildings and materials for use as history laboratories.

Obviously, we have been brought to a point in time where all of our educational and museum history forces us to consider abandoning the outmoded old in favor of the promising new. In the words of the old seaman, "The time to put on sail is when you feel a breeze." Then perhaps we shall realize the objectives enunciated by the Congress of the United States when, in passinng the legislation that established the National Foundation of the Arts and the Humanities, it declared "that Democracy demands wisdom and vision in its citizens and that it must therefore foster and support a form of education designed to make them masters of their technology and not its unthinking servant" and "that a high civilization must not limit its efforts to science and technology alone but must give full values and support to the other great branches of man's scholarly and cultural activity." It just might be that they were referring to you and to me.

▲   ▲   ▲

ANOTHER VOICE:
ENGLISH AND THE HUMANITIES

BENJAMIN DEMOTT

I MAY have misassessed your interests and your concerns, but my first notion was that the interest of having somebody like me—what's called an Ivy League English Prof—come and speak to people who teach secondary school and elementary school pupils would be that perhaps the man would answer a question; or say something relevant to the pressures that are felt by people in secondary schools nowadays, particularly people who are concerned about getting some of their students into Ivy League colleges. The question—What should we do with the Humanities?—has meaning for many people who teach largely in terms of getting somebody into something. For us who teach in college the problem is to get somebody into a graduate school. For people teaching in secondary schools the problem is to get people into all colleges—into all courses.

There is a certain kind or rhetoric that we make in Ivy League schools at this moment. We say, "No, we really are not terribly interested in scores any more; we don't really believe in S.A.T. and we are trying to get out of the rate race of 700-over 700. We don't really think it's terribly important for everybody to have an enormously high verbal aptitude. Really what we are looking for is"—and then comes the real rhetoric—"Character, spontaneity, individuality, unique approach, someone with lopsided interests. We want somebody who can play the contra bassoon and play in very, very well, and if that person can't tell a Bunsen burner from Leonardo de Vinci, well, we'll fix that person up when he comes to town." There is a certain sort of new style rhetoric which is anti-examination; but then again and again, when people *without* high verbal aptitude and *without* high S.A.T. achievement are presented as candidates for institutions of my sort, they fair badly. They're turned down and they may be valedictorians and so on, but the assumption is that perhaps we could get somebody who's very, very apt verbally and also is unique, spontaneous, splendid and full of character and full of energy. To a degree, in short, we haven't got quite yet the courage of our new found publicly proclaimed standards and as a result, the revolution, the significant curriculum reform, is slowed down because there is nervousness in the secondary school. Nervousness about whether institutions like mine are serious in their proclamations about not caring anymore, not caring as much as they once cared, about students being prepared in the sense of having their native abilities as talkers and as writers highly developed before they arrive.

Teachers in secondary schools still feel under pressure, especially teachers who are trying to get students into Ivy League colleges. By the same token we who are in college feel under extreme pressure from the graduate schools for, as everyone knows, 60 or 70 or 80 percent of all students do go on to graduate school. And the task is, as we say, to get them into a good one, not to fail the student, and some way to prepare him for a professional career even while he is an undergraduate. Thus the highest praise for some of us, the highest praise we are to understand at least, comes from the graduate school teacher at the university who says to our student or says to us, sometimes in a letter, "Yes, I am delighted to take the man you've just recommended; we are delighted to admit him because our experience with your students has been that they are ready to do the second year of graduate level work, not the first year, when they come to us. We are delighted at the marvelous way that you are preparing students in your undergraduate liberal arts institution for the graduate school. Indeed, some of your people in English Literature—or some of your people in Economics—have really finished the first year of graduate school before they get to us, and bully for you," they say. "Bully for you because you're doing a marvelous job." The question is, is it the job of the teacher forever to prepare people for some other school, to labor at getting somebody into another school?

A good teacher at the college level is intensely resentful of the graduate school teacher whose high compliment to the undergraduate teacher is that the man that's just been sent is an apt person for professionalized, specialized study. The best praise of the undergraduate teacher would lie in some other direction, just as I think the best praise of you is not that when the students leave they are acquainted with what we call trad, the trad of English literature, or the trad of history. The tradition. They know the past; they've heard of Shakespeare and they even know about the Grecian Urn. So that's not the right praise for a teacher. It's very hard, as I say, to keep this in mind, hard for me to keep it in mind in my position, very hard for teachers at secondary-primary levels to keep it in mind.

What conception of teaching the humanities should a teacher have no matter where he is? No matter whether he is a secondary school teacher or an undergraduate teacher in a college or a graduate school teacher. I think he's beyond redemption so committed is he to scientizing the subject, so committed is he to turning our subject—the humanities—into a body of knowledge. That last phrase makes it quite plain I will start by saying we must above all be resistant to the notion that the humanities constitutes a body of knowledge which can be summed up as knowledge of art, knowledge of literature, and knowledge of music. Our subject is not Shakespeare. The English teacher's subject is not Shakespeare; and it is not Keats and Shelley, and it is not the Romantic Movement. If I am an American literature teacher my subject is not Melville, is not Faulkner. I need not know anything about the Transcendentalists and I need not spend most of my time trying to make people know something about the Transcendentalists. My subject, as a teacher of the humanities, is *human objects and human situations*.

That's what art is for: to make things—human things, human relations, human situations—palpable to men. We have students before us who are virtually blind to experience. They move in a world, relatively speaking, as yet unnamed for them in human terms. Perhaps they can make some guesses about what is there in the way of human forms, what is there in the way of possible human relations, what is there in the way of possible kinds of character. They know little and in order to know more we have art. We have literary art, we have pictures, we have plays, we have poems. The proper teacher of the humanities is a person who is always, always ready to sacrifice the art to the object the

75

art purports to clarify, purports to comment on, purports to make real to the student. Our subject should never be construed, never be regarded historically for the sake of history. It should be regarded historically, when? Why? For the reason of showing what human objects and human situations have been at other moments. For the purpose of doing what? Knowing about those other moments? No, not finally. In order to help our student know who he is and what the nature of his situation is. There is no history independently interesting.

By the same token, our interests should never be to persuade students to think of art in terms of better and worse. No teaching going on in America or in England today is worse than the teaching that depends upon what's called the "taste test"; or that says it aims to improve, to elevate the taste of the student by doing what is called "exposing him to good lit." You don't expose people to good lit in order to improve their taste; you don't expose them to bad lit in order to corrupt their taste. Your aim always is to use the book, use the object, use the poem —whatever it is—to clarify experience. To make something the students like palpable that probably was not palpable before. The minute we institute the kind of teaching that says, "Students, here are two poems and one is dreadful and one is very good, and the assignment is to tell us which is the good poem," we say that the subject—the central theme of the humanities— is that "x" poem is better than "y" poem, that what is interesting about art is that some art is better than other art. What a dreadful reduction of the art of our subject! Always we have to have at the center of our teaching enterprise the notion that it is the human object and the human situation that art is meant to serve, that literary art is meant to serve. Always we begin away from art. We begin away from the poem and move from student experience to a text and then never, never stay there but always try at the end to move back out of the text, back into life itself. These are very abstract observations and don't have too much meaning until some attempt is made to say, "What exactly do you propose that a teacher do with a particular text? How do you teach a poem?"

Recently while going about and talking at conferences I have discovered that about the second day of the conference people say, "We've had an awful lot *about* teaching, why don't we *do* some teaching now?" Instead of all this rhetoric why don't we break up into small groups of five and six and choose a common text and each one take five minutes to say what he would do." When that happens sometimes you see the relative emptiness of "x's" platitudes and the relative fullness of a class prepared by a man who cannot describe what it is that he wishes to do but who, nevertheless, can bloody well teach. This is a common difficulty—the difficulty of a good teacher in saying precisely what it is that he does. More and more at conferences people seem to be ready and willing to show off their teaching one to another, but the curious thing at such conferences is the long time spent clearing the air, getting down to teaching. At a recent conference when we broke to do a poem and spent our little time in session, four or five of us talking in turn about a poem, we came to realize that most people who teach the humanities tend to work out strategies to avoid saying what they do as teachers. They work out ways of saying, "I don't think we should have chosen this poem" or "I don't know this poem very well; I'll talk about another poem and you people talk about the one that has been assigned"—the various ploys by which the teacher gets off, gets out of facing this very difficult situation of matching what you want to do as a teacher with what somebody else wants to do.

When we talked about a poem at one conference we used "The Man He Killed" by Thomas Hardy.

I thought you might be interested in hearing some of the words people said when we came into session. Everybody said "The first thing I do with a poem is read it in class, that's the first thing I do, read it." Then the question was whether you would have the student read the poem or you, the teacher, read the poem? And would you read it once or twice? Would you have them read it once or twice? What would you do? And so on. Now usually in conversation about how to teach the class I'd say at least five or ten minutes was spent by teachers on this very, very, very significant question of reading the poem. How exactly would you read the poem? Most people (once arriving on agreement that it would probably be better for everybody to read the poem, you see—the students could read it, the teacher could read it, and if there was a custodian in the hall, he could read it!) work it out that we certainly wanted to know what the poem was. The common assumption seemed to be we would then face it as a poem; that is to say, we would say, "Well, this 'The Man He Killed'—this is by Thomas Hardy and it is a poem and we could call it a war poem, and so on." Then we would say, "What do you think of it, students? What do you think of it?" And possibly at that moment the students would have an an opinion. If they didn't the teacher would drag out his teaching artillery; namely, the ways in which one could talk about the poem, the things one could say about the poem, who is talking in the poem, what is the speaker in the poem like, how do the various elements of the poem connect, what about those rhymes. There are rhymes, are they? Yes! Yes! There are rhymes; and, and what does *nipperkin* mean, eh? And rush off to the dictionary, usually to find that old nipperkin wasn't in the dictionary. You have to get some special book, clear up the hard words and work out those very difficult elisions, as for example, "he thought he'd 'list, perhaps." What's that? "list?" Well, you know, "list" sort of means . . . but here it doesn't. It means "enlist," you see, and so on.

By the time fifteen minutes had passed by you've got an impression of what would happen in most English teachers' classes with this poem. There would be a tremendous interest in something called the poem, the text, but no clarity about why anybody should be, or would be, interested in looking at this object to begin with, the assumption being that the poem would earn its way because it was a poem; that works of art earn their way because they are works of art. The student—poor wretch—knows that he must treat the poem with respect because he picks that mannerism up from his teacher.

It seemed to me very plain what you would oppose in this sort of teaching. You'd not start the class by talking about the poem at all; you'd not say one word about the poem. A good

English teacher doesn't start his classes by reading a poem, no more than a good teacher of fine arts starts his classes by putting something up on the screen and saying, "Ha! Ha! Here's Giorgione and here's 'A Picnic.' Now, look students." A good teacher would begin far outside the poem. He would begin by having made for himself the choice of a subject, having decided what it was that he wanted to talk about with students that day. He would launch himself on a conversation about what? Well, about a human situation, a human problem, a human difficulty, or a human success. He would launch himself on a subject about which he was fairly certain his students, even in their primitive rude shape, would have opinions and would have an interest. He would begin his class by talking with his students about what we call life. Now not undisciplined talk. Instantly people worry and say, "Well, about life, it's a lower subject." It would be life under a particular rubric.

What would be the appropriate rubric for the person who had decided that he wanted to talk also in class that day about "The Man He Killed"? Now those of you who know the poem know that a fairly appropriate subject might be war and why we fight. Why we fight; what we say to each other to make it clear to ourselves; what human beings say to each other to make clear to themselves the notion of the enemy—the notion of the enemy who must be contained, or knocked off, ruined, despised, or whatever. How do we make this experience—this experience of saying, "Our country has an enemy,"—real to ourselves? One might then, as an English teacher, begin his conversation by asking questions about what one thought about our present enemy. How did we learn to see the enemy as the enemy? How do we know the enemy as the enemy? A very simple word, what is the enemy anyway? How many people here have seen the enemy? How many people have a personal knowledge of what it is we are fighting?

Presumably we don't want to spend the whole class this way. We want to spend a part of the class this way because if we don't spend part of the class this way, what then will the class be when the poem enters? The poem will be a text coming from the moon; the poem will not be seen as in truth what it is: what all works of art are, yet another voice in the room. I turn to the poem after ten or fifteen minutes of conversation in order that there be one other voice in the room—not mine and not my students—and a voice talking in such a way that it can be felt to be part of a conversation already going on. One of the most difficult things about any kind of art is the way in which it comes. We forget it now—those of us who've studied it are always forgetting it—the way it comes before people in a "ripped from its context" way. The poem is there. You thrust it before students and all its surroundings are not there. "Behold yon solitary reaper," says Wordsworth, and the fair-minded person says, Where? Who? What? Why? When? And under what circumstances? Why should anybody look at her? And what is a reaper and what is a highland and what is yon? And why behold a farm worker—just as a peasant? And so on. The "all of before" of a poem is invisible just as all the surroundings of the work of art are ruled out. I look at my Rouault Crucifixion and I say, "Well, what came before? Why should the Christ figure on the cross look simply tired and not racked and not haunted and not pained?"

In order to make up the picture, in order to make up the poem, I have to have something going around it. The teacher's job is to make that stuff that goes around the poem before the poem is ever there. Then, then, then, I can read the poem. It's immaterial whether I read it or they read it, and anyone who says they must always read or that I must always read is, I think, quite mad. You simply want to say, "Well, when it's conversation we'll let anybody into the conversation. If you want to take up the role of the poem talker, go ahead; take it up. If you don't want to, I'll take it up." So we look at the poem and what does it say?

"The Man He Killed"*

by Thomas Hardy

"Had he and I but met
By some old ancient inn,
We should have sat us down to wet
Right many a nipperkin!

"But ranged as infantry,
And staring face to face
I shot at him as he at me,
And killed him in his place.

"I shot him dead because—
Because he was my foe,
Just so—my foe of course he was;
That's clear enough; although

"He thought he'd 'list, perhaps,
Off-hand like—just as I—
Was out of work—had sold his traps—
No other reason why.

"Yes; quaint and curious war is!
You shoot a fellow down
You'd treat if met where any bar is,
Or help to half-a-crown."

*Collected Poems of Thomas Hardy, Macmillan, 1926.

Then having gone through the poem reading it you say, "Well, what's he talking about? What's he saying about enemies? What's the center of his interest about the enemy?" What one is trying to say is very simple: what the poem does, what the work of literary art does is take the student where? Into the experience, back into the moment. Poetry is very reductive and art is very reductive. It's all particulars; it's all moment-to-moment experience. Art is the wheel on which the abstractions are broken. They're broken here by a simple man, a simple man who's saying, "Well, he was my enemy, and I don't know how much I can say about this experience except that it's puzzling, that's all. He was just a man, that's all."

Now, what one wants to do as one talks with students at this point is to bring them inside the experience of this kind of human encounter, among all the kinds of human encounter there are. The human encounter between the enemies—that first of all. But then beyond that there's another encounter much more interesting in a poem, and that is the encounter between a person talking in the poem and the person he is talking to. Because there is somebody being talked to here, somebody listening to the story, presumably somebody younger.

Now at this point in my talk with students about the poem, I step back again and say, "Let's put the poem out of sight." I don't bother to say that; I just look away from the poem and I say, "Tell us something about a meeting you've had with a stranger lately. Where have you met one?" With my students very often it's hitchhiking or sometimes it's on boats going across the ocean in the summertime, or something like that, but every student has met a stranger. What one is interested in talking about now is the question how do you make contact with a stranger? What do you say? Who usually starts talking? What does a stranger say? What kinds of things does he say? How do you talk when you're a stranger talking to somebody else? Who initiates the conversation? You start talking about hitchhiking—who talks first? Well, the person who drives the car usually invites the conversation, and there's a convention here that says that if he doesn't invite conversation usually the rider keeps his mouth shut too. There is a whole set of conversations that you can have: where you were born, where you go to school, what you're doing, and so on. Here you're doing something called making a contact, human connection, one person with the next. Then we try in short to say what we're doing in this conversation. What the teacher is aiming to do is to establish for the student some consciousness of the ways in which human connection is made and to establish that this too is an experience, the meeting of strangers, and that there are conditions of feeling that exist here that don't exist in any other moment—that one's performance in a meeting as a stranger can be better and more human if one knows what sort of situation one is in. "Now what sort of situation is the man in here at the bar?" Then come back to the poem.

What sort of situation is this? Who is he talking to and what is it likely that he's doing? As I listen to him I can see what he's doing. He's drawing attention to himself. He's saying, "I, I killed a man." He is, as it were, making himself into a significant person by telling a story, which is a common enough human thing to do, but the question is how do we feel when someone ruminates in this way upon some central remembered experience of his own? How do we feel when people do this to us, make a narrative, say, "This was an odd and puzzling experience. I killed a man. I looked him in the eye and then I killed him." How does this make us feel? In a way the man is putting us on a bit, just slightly, making us into an audience; and the question is, why do human beings make other human beings into audiences? Perhaps out of desire to probe for some kind of answer to a mystery that troubles them. What mystery? The mystery of unconnection; here—unconnected human beings. The mystery that turns human beings into enemies. The enemy, the person seen ranged as infantry face to face, is not so very much different finally from the stranger listening to the tale in the bar. One doesn't know exactly what the other human being is; therefore, he can as easily be persuaded—we can as easily be persuaded—to regard him as an enemy as we can be persuaded to regard him as our audience. Well, I imitated the class badly, but you can't do a class well, you know, unless it's a class.

But the point is that one talks to this poem, as to any poem, as to any picture, always in the hope of talking to something beyond the poem and one always chooses works of art. One is going to do, as we say, with students purely and almost wholly on the basis of what kind of talk the student can make back to that work of art from the conversation that you begin with. The perpetual aim of the teacher is to say the work of art does not count as a thing itself. It counts only as an illumination. The work of art is not our subject, no more than literary history is our subject, no more than literary criticism is our subject. Our subject is always the imaginative life of the student; we want him to speculate on the world; we want him to speculate upon human relations; we want him to use art for those things that art is so marvelously capable of being used for—namely, to give point and penetration to his observations of life and experience.

▲   ▲   ▲

Q. The materials in the book are not organized this way.

A. They are indeed not organized this way. And I think the teacher has to be brutal in his disregard of the kind of organization that he is offered. For example, the organization in most literary texts is one of two or three different kinds. There is formal organization. We will do the poem; we will do the story; we will do the play; we will do the comedy; we will do the tragedy, and so on. There's that sort of possibility. There's the lyric, hmm? There's pastoral poetry. There are bits of epic—da dum, da dum, da dum, da dum—and we want you students to know the difference between the lyric and the heroic couplet; and we want you to know a sonnet when you walk up to it and look at it. The first thing that you should think when you see a sonnet is Ooooh! A sonnet! That's one mode of organization. Another mode of organization is historical and there it's very important that we should know that Shelley comes after Shakespeare because "e" comes after "a", you see, and so on. And you should remember that because history matters tremendously.

The first thing that you think of when you see "The Rape of the Lock" by Alexander Pope is 1726, 1727, 1735, or whatever it is —I can't remember myself; I'm ashamed.

But the point is that the good teacher has the courage to take the book by the throat. He takes the text by the throat and says, "Look, I am not going to be intimidated by the theory of literary form, just as I'm not going to be intimidated by the question what's good and what's bad. I'm only going to be intimidated by my sense of what my role as a human being is, and my distinct role as a human being, as a teacher of the humanities, is to do something for the imaginative life of my students." What that means is give them what chance literature can give them to probe into experience, to look into life as far as their eyes at their age can take them, to fall into the habit of speculating upon human relations, to fall into the habit of having experience. You don't have experience indeed until you ask yourself what is it that's going on. The answer to the question—what about the book?—is to be vigorous, rough, brutal and resentful of the book and make it serve your end.

Q. Wouldn't the scientific approach be to have a person read the poem who could really give it everything it's supposed to have, versus the human approach of everybody reading it differently? The people listening would have a much greater appreciation of the poem.

A. I would say always that the reading I'm interested in is the reading that the individual student can make of the poem. While it is true that the poem can be well served by a good reader, when your aim is to serve the poem you forget your aim as a teacher. Your aim as a teacher is to take everyone in the class into the inward life of that poem, as far as he or she can go into the experience. That's why I think the talk about shall we read it or shall we not read it, who shall read it, shall the teacher read it, shall we get the thing there before us to be quite niggling. It's not the central question to ask about what you do in the classroom. The important thing to say is, "How can I get students in the humanities classroom into the world of reflection and speculation where they can begin to experience the difference and the mystery of politics as separating man from man?" That's very mysterious, how political organization—these are not words I'd say in my class, but that's really finally what the poem is somehow about—it's about this whole general area in which we human beings make up distinctions among ourselves that are so vital to us that we can only see their relative triviality. Once we are back in face to face combat with the other fellow we realize, my God, I am shooting another man because of the difference between Marxism and something else, Communism and something else.

Q. I don't see why your discussions would not be served by a good reading of the poem because the whole thing is distorted if the student doesn't read it correctly. Then the personal meaning of the poem doesn't become clear in the comments of the discussion. That's what you want.

A. No. I hate to contradict you, but that's not what I most want. I'm not most concerned, I'm not most interested in getting the meaning of the poem across. The poem—this is a terrible thing to say—but the poem is expendable. The work of art is expendable and the meaning, the particular meaning, of the work of art is highly expendable too. It would be nice if we could in a classroom pull together fifteen or twenty, let's say, ordinary high school sophomores into some sort of very perceptive and acute understanding of these precise particulars of this poem. That would be marvelous, but I don't think it's ever been done. I've tried, I've been trying to do that for years in classrooms with college students; never succeed in doing it. There's always half the class outside the poem talking about something else. Now the question is can we have at least the whole class thinking and talking in the same general area, speculating in the same general area? The poem does not exist for itself and we don't exist for the poem. Just as art does not exist for itself and we just don't exist for art. All the energy here is an energy that goes toward the world, that tries to seize upon experience and clarify that. So if they don't do justice to the poem in their reading and do, nevertheless, come to some sort of hesitant comprehension of this particular mystery—the mystery of the gap between political division and human solidarity —I think it's relatively immaterial whether Hardy comes off well or not.

Q. But you do want to understand the poem as a springboard for discussion don't you?

A. No. the poem is another voice in that discussion. The teacher of the Humanities is supposed to be not a person whose great understanding is of Shakespeare as literature; he's supposed to be a person who has some understanding of life itself. That's what our claim is. A claim not to knowledge exactly in the academic sense. What we're supposed to be is people who are accustomed to speculating, imagining, brooding, probing facts of experience.

Q. I have had the experience of first reading Shakespeare on my own and then seeing the Shakespeare play performed correctly. The performance, or the proper reading of a poem, illuminates the meaning.

A. I'm not denying that for a moment. Yes, everything should be performed; yes, everything should be well read ideally. There is no question but that a good doing of a Shakespeare play makes things much more living to students; it makes its meaning clear. What I'm saying, though, is that my subject is still not the meaning of Shakespeare; that's not what I'm primarily engaged in doing and thinking about as a teacher.

Q. Would it probably be true from your method that a student would be more perceptive than a teacher, more perceptive than before?

A. He might inwardly become so. Whether or not he became a better reader of poems would be, relatively speaking again, not nearly as important as whether he fell into the habit of speculating about the course of his movement through life. It's hard to speak to this subject without saying something about the relative blankness with which most people—myself included —pass through their experience. Most days are not experience at all. We're traveling at perpetual "between"; we're on our way from Amherst to Detroit, and in a moment I'll be on my way from Detroit to Amherst. That sense of always being on an arch, of always never living, never living in time as though there were an age to time, but always living as though, "Soon I will start living, soon I will start speculating, soon I will start doing something." And when will I start doing that? It turns out for most people that the moment when they might speculate about life is that moment when they prepare a class. That's when I'm most living and am most inclined to do the thing that I wish my students were doing always. I don't mean to be some windy platitudinous character, but I think we are at our best as human beings when we are doing what we call gossip; when we try to probe into the motives of other human beings for doing what they do. When I say at our best, I say at our most human. This is what an imagination is for, to care and to attend to life and to explore life. Most people don't do much of that.

Q. Would you give us a lesson using one of Rembrandt's self-portraits or one of Beethoven's syphonies?

A. It's not too difficult to do what I'm talking about with pictures—hard with abstract pictures but not impossible even with them. With music the task is very much more complicated. What you try to do with a picture is to rule out the same kind of talk that I try to rule out in discussions of a poem.

At a recent conference a teacher of the fine arts put up on the screen the Giorgione picture I mentioned before—"The Picnickers", the two naked ladies and the two clothed men. Then he read from a student paper written the first day of the course: "I don't see what this picture is for really, and I don't like it, and why are the ladies naked and the men clothed and what is Giorgione getting at?" Ho hum—that was about the end. Then the teacher read a paper written six weeks later after his students had been through the fine arts mill and the picture under discussion was one by Rouault. Flashing the Rouault on the screen the teacher began reading from the student paper something like this: "Notice how the light draws the eye to the center of the picture and how your eye now travels up to the left and now travels back to the center—central light—and

88

then up to the right." And so on. What the student had managed to do was turn the picture into a road map but he was using what is called the "critical language of the fine arts." And the teacher who was describing this was tapping himself on the back and promoting himself for having, as he said, given the student a beginning knowledge of how to express his experience of a work of art.

What is the point of doing pictures of this sort with students? You should try to talk about the life of feeling in the picture, the kinds of human relations that are set up within the picture. You should not try constantly to empty pictures of their human substance. Nevertheless, the mode of fine arts teaching, as is true of the mode of poetry teaching at the moment, is one which does empty works of their human content. It rules out the notion that the function of art is to clarify and to speculate and to probe for us about human situations, human objects and so on.

As for music, much more difficult. One thing that one conceivably can do with students as a beginning ploy is just to consider how the life of a cadence determines for the listener the conditions of his feeling. If I play a leading chord I set up expectations. If those expectations are not satisfied—let's say, if I don't go sooner or later to the tonic, to the rest—I then feel within me some sort of complicated agitation. How am I going to name that agitation? How am I going to name the condition of feeling within me? That's a problem a teacher can begin with. And why begin here? Because the feeling, the agitation, the unrested, the unfinished sense of experience there that's created at moments within a piece of music, the anticipations and the anxieties that are created by "unfinishedness" in music are like some agitations and unfinishedness, some anxieties in experience itself. We would not be as responsive to music as we are if it were without human contact; if it did not, as we say, speak to our feelings in the language the feelings understand. Well, that's not my subject and I shouldn't have even said that much.

89

Q. How do you handle the time element in something such as this?

A. By the time element, do you mean the length of classes and what you have to cover?

Q. Yes. Is this a problem in your teaching? Are you on a schedule of some sort?

A. Yes, I'm on a schedule. But it's much easier for a college teacher than it is for other teachers because he always makes his own schedule. The force, the thrust of the Humanities now should be to say "Do not give me a schedule, do not tell me that there is anything in my subject that demands coverage." There is no coverage in our subject. There is nothing, nothing that people *need* to know. If I am teaching literature there is no obligation whatever on my part to, as we say, acquaint them with one play of Shakespeare or two plays of Shakespeare or something like that. That is not the aim of the teacher. Our field is not to acquaint people with objective works standing out there separate from them. It is to provide a place where for forty minutes or an hour the mind and imagination of the child can work in a way it cannot work any place else in the curriculum—freely, speculatively without doing anymore than making experience real to itself. Elsewhere subjects have what we call content and elsewhere it is appropriate for students to be told there are certain concepts they must master. It is not appropriate in the humanities and arts classroom, not at all.

Q. Do we teach the Humanities? It seems to me that we don't; that the humanities is a method of teaching, a philosophy of the individual teacher, whether teaching art or whether teaching math or social studies.

A. That's entirely right as far as I'm concerned. The teacher of the humanities is a person who has a conception of the individual student, who has a conception of human needs and human interests. And he has within him some experience and some capacity for articulate expression, articulate consciousness of what humanness is. He uses the arts, history, philosophy and religion—these inventions of man—to help him articulate and

90

to help other articulate their consciousness of their experience. That is what is going on in the Humanities ideally.

Q. How do you evaluate whether this is happening in class. The students might soak it up but how do you find out?

A. That's a first rate question. I hate to sound as though I'm against everything, but in humanities teaching I'm afraid I am. The whole impulse to evaluate performance in our classrooms is by and large a bad impulse. All attempts at measurement of performance in the humanities are corrupting. It doesn't matter whether they are S.A.T. verbal aptitude tests or whether they are examinations on set tests, they all work in the same way. What they do is suggest to the students that what he does when he confronts the humanities is something like what he does when he confronts an ordinary body of knowledge. And it is not like that at all.

Q. But it seems to me that if you are teaching a humanities course you need to know if you are reaching the student.

A. And how can you know? The question is a good one and, it is painful to say, virtually unanswerable. The way you'll find out will be a negative finding out. Most young people, college students, have not yet fallen into the habit of speculating in a lively way on experience. They do not regard that kind of use of the mind as one that's natural to them. I suppose the way to determine success here would be to wait for a generation and see whether you had any lively eyes among the young people. It would be as simple as that. I don't think we've got many lively eyes. Now even in our brightest students there is some kind of blankness before the face of experience which seems to me to be evidence that the humanities teacher, myself included, has not been doing his job.

Q. How would you prevent a new "American Studies" course from becoming illustrated American history?

A. When it comes to matters of history the points that one would make are fairly commonplace. They are articles of faith among all the people who have been responsible for curriculum reform in the social sciences. We now are fairly convinced that we don't want a study of history that will consider history to be an objective collection of knowledge or bits of information which the student masters. We want the student to have a sense of history like his hoped-for sense of poetry. That is to say, history is a means by which I can place myself in the world. History is a means by which I can come to an understanding of my relation to other people within my community. The aim should be to develop problems in American Studies that can be understood by students as offering ways of making their daily experience more comprehensible to them—their walk to and from school, the objects their eyes encounter along the way. One way we have of making what happens to us more comprehensible is by understanding its precedence, by understanding what came before it. But if I had to scrap chronology for an immediate project, I would.

Q. What should be done about the fine arts in the elementary school?

A. The best thing that I've ever read about teaching art in elementary school is a book by an English lady named Sybil Marshall called *An Experiment in Education*. It's available in paperback, a Cambridge University Press book. Sybil Marshall is a teacher in a one-teacher school running from first grade all the way up though what we would call tenth grade. She is a marvelous art teacher. She uses art (and I believe in this use of pictures) to enable people who are not articulate in words use pictures to express their experience, their family experience, for instance. People who are less apt at telling you about the organization of life within the family in words can sometimes tell you a lot in pictures. One of the things that Mrs. Marshall so brilliantly does in that book, which has student pictures in it, is compare student essays about family life and student pictures about family life.

The right use of art in the elementary school is again to clarify immediate experience. You don't invite people to do pictures of the moon and of the stars, of objects unrelated to immediate experience. You try to encourage the students from the very beginning to see art as a way of putting before himself facts of his own immediate experience that are significant to him. There is a whole world of activities that is real in his life but, conceivably, may not exist for him until he tries to express it.

Q. Do you accept, then, the child trying to draw anything?

A. No. I think the teacher has to be prescriptive to a degree. She has to have a subject. The teacher has to start the conversation in a particular area, something like the way I start talking about a poem.

Q. Would you let her take time to teach proportion?

A. When there is a human reason for knowing proportion.

Q. This gentleman wants to draw a picture of his mother and dad. Are you going to take time prior to that to teach proportion?

A. No. You start with the humanness; you start with a need; you start with a desire to represent. Then if that representation can be improved in a way that you see will be more satisfactory to the child, more in accordance with what the child wishes to express, then yes. You are not teaching proportion but teaching a way of enabling the child to say what he wishes to say and has a need to say about his experience. We're not after developing craftsman-like skills. The aim is not to develop the skill for the sake of the skill any more than the aim is to read the poem correctly for the sake of the poem. The aim is to put the child in a position to do what he wishes to do in the way of expression, to meet his need for expression.

Q. Should I teach shadowing, proportion, depth perception first or should I let them express themselves first.

A. What is the point of knowing how to do something if you do not wish to know how to do it? The best art teaching I have seen is the teaching of Mrs. Marshall and she begins with the need. She does not teach skills in order that some non-existent need that may come into existence after the skills have

93

been developed can be met. She starts with a need and if there is no need, then the child doesn't do art in her class. Just as simple as that.

Q. When we say that children who can't write well maybe can paint well, are we saying art is a kind of second fiddle to literature?

A. Not at all.

Q. The literature people in the humanities like to think it's all a means of expression of some social aspect around them. But what about the arts that simply express the relationship between red and green? If we let Johnny draw about mother and sister we're selling him short about what is going on contemporarily in the arts, about the relationship between a triangle and a square.

A. That's true. That is what I am prepared to sell short momentarily. I'm prepared to sell that kind of knowledge in literature and in the arts too. I think we can buy it back later. College is the place to buy it back. The problem is that students come to college already convinced the the world of education, the world of the school and the world of art, are worlds essentially unrelated to their experience, essentially unrelated to human experience. There is nothing that I as a single teacher can do against that. That is a whole complicated acculturation that begins in the school because of the fundamental unreality of Humanities teaching all the way through from the first grade right through college as well.

THE ARTS AND THE HUMANITIES: AN EXPANDING UNIVERSE

HAROLD HAYDON

THE ESSENTIAL unity of the arts together with their breadth, afford the best guarantee that the growing prominence of the arts in the fields of the humanities will work to unify the approach to humanistic disciplines despite the tendency to insularity of these disciplines.

The trend to unity of viewpoint appears obvious, however difficult it may seem to cross disciplinary lines in the shadow of the age of specialization. That age has ended now, and the more alert and aggressive disciplines, the sciences, are aware of the fact while their erstwhile counterparts, the humanities, are slow to realize the new condition. When some time ago the Massachusetts Institute of Technology in a curriculum revision made more room for the humanities in the education of scientists and engineers, it did not seem a great concession to humanists, but was significant of a changing attitude. The dedicated scientist is expected to have some acquaintance with the humanities, not only for the good of his soul, but in hope that humane values will color and inform his work.

On the side of the humanities, efforts usually center on preserving the liberal and polite studies associated with culture against further inroads of technology and science. One takes it for granted that students of the humanities will get their full share of science as penance for being born into this world, but do humanists make efforts to integrate the sciences and the humanities? to establish and encourage a dialogue? to let one inform the other? It must be rarely so. Old habits of defense, of world aplenty to explore in this our dewdrop, in short, habits of specialization, preclude the liberating cross ferilization of art and science. "What has that to do with us?" is the refrain of the confirmed specialist, of the scholar for whom his cell of learning is the whole world, unlit by any window into farther fields.

If book-learning and cultivation of the polite arts of appreciation were all of the humanities, the cell might hold the scholar, and the islands of learning their castaways, in happy insularity. But the creative and performing arts literally have burst upon the American scene since Franklin Delano Roosevelt inaugurated the first American Art Week with a plea to Americans to notice the arts, and the boy down the street who may be an artist. These arts are not confined to books and often are not polite. They have a tough reality about them: the string must be struck to sound the tone; paint must be manipulated to produce the painting; stone and metal must be cut with steel or fire or lasers to make the sculpture; words must be marshalled to make the poem; coordinates in time and space are necessary for the dance. Above all, the arts remain the freest of man's activities, invite the unexpected interchange, and refuse to be categorized. They deal in the crudest stuff of the earth and through it touch the stars. If anything can wake up the sleeping humanities it will be the lively arts. If anything can bridge the gap between the humanities and the sciences it is art. The arts can serve as means whereby a humane point of view may supersede the unitary disciplinary approach.

This is not to advocate some mystical or magical overview—a supra-appreciation of arts and letters. There can be no separate discipline called the Humanities. The blight on the arts in the humanities has been "art appreciation", a detached dilettantism that repels the healthy mind. There can be nothing easy or simple about a humane point of view. While it may be human-centered and broadly inclusive, the viewpoint is based on knowledge and knowledge is to be found in the various disciplines of the arts. To adopt a "humanities point of view" one must keep close contacts with the specific disciplines and participate rather than observe.

For an example of what this means in practice, I turn to an experiment begun over 20 years ago in which I had a part, when an integrated humanities course was organized in the College of the University of Chicago, uniting the study of the plastic arts, music, and literature in a single year-long sequence. Common features of these arts provided the basic plan for the course, starting with the relation of art to nature, followed by the "elements" of art, music, and literature, principles of organization, the role of materials and techniques, the artist and his works, schools and traditions in art, and for a final fillip, "contemporary trends". Addressing lectures, demonstrations, and discussions to these topics, each art was taken up in turn for a week, sometimes for two weeks.

The initial staff of three, the artist, the musician, and the poet, expanded to include others, each qualified in one of these fields and sometimes in two. Week by week, the experts in the arts under discussion gave the general lecture and briefed the staff, while all members led discussion groups in what must have been one of the most demanding yet truly educative of tasks. The artist sweated as much over the intricacies of time, tempo, and rhythm as the musician sweated over the distinctions between relief, intaglio, and planographic prints, yet with time and good students course content and methods increased and improved; slides, reproductions, and records were supplemented by original art in the classroom, use of the Art Institute of Chicago, and live concerts on campus.

In these beginning years students were cautioned against making value judgements too soon and were urged first to look at the plastic arts, listen to music, and read poetry and prose perceptively. They were not asked to describe their emotions; they were asked to state what they saw and heard, and to talk about these experiences in language appropriate to each art. Precisely because it is easy in a cross-blending of experience in the arts to blur important distinctions, language was invoked in disciplinary terms. The word "color" has one group of meanings for art, another for music, and yet another for literature; so it is also with "line", "tone", and other terms.

The common or basic patterns of the arts were examined without losing sight of the special qualities of each art, and students were led as far as possible into each; in some fields this included work in the art. Testing revealed that students became sufficiently involved and interested in architecture to follow this art beyond the limits of the course, testing higher later on than at the end of the course. Tests also showed that students who studied the arts in the context of this course where names and dates were not important, actually learned more names and dates than students in courses geared to emphasize those facts.

I would underline my belief that there can be no valid overview of the humanities that sweeps up the arts in generalities. Instead the humane viewpoint is valid when it respects the disciplines of art in their own terms, yet, through knowledge of all, senses their basic unities—unities stemming from common sources in human experience, a need for balance, for variety, for flow, and pause, and termination.

In the training of the creative artist it is certain that he never can be too broadly educated. There is nothing that an artist may not turn to account in his art and nothing that he need not know. Great artists in all fields of art have been great humanists and there really is no adequate preparation for the artist that is segregated and strictly technical, or limited to one art alone.

Similarly, for general education, no narrow specializations are acceptable now. The youth, troubled by the uncertainities, relative conclusions, and open-endedness of inquiries in the arts because he has been led to assume the finality and conclusiveness of science, must travel further in science to learn that, there too, final answers can be assumed and that creative scientists, like creative artists, manipulate their materials with a combination of practicality and intuition, experiencing similar aesthetic rewards in the pursuit of their respective arts. His acquaintance with the arts will make this realization possible.

Nor is this association of the arts and sciences only a romantic notion. Swiftly developing technical and material innovations make it inevitable that the artist will collaborate with the scientist and that lines between art and science, between the humanities and the sciences, will blur and obliterate. As a simple illustration, at the very birth of Op art Gerald Oster mounted an exhibition of standard textbook optical illusions, moiré patterns, lens refractions, and other known effects, beautifully executed and displayed. The exhibit quite clearly charmed the public, aware mainly of the optical play of the new art, and Oster may be regarded as one who with a minimum of creation, confined largely to packaging the effects, nevertheless laid the cornerstones for much that followed from the hands and minds of artists interested in using, instead of merely stating, these optical facts and their consequences.

For the past year there has been an informal association in New York City of a number of technicians in optics, lighting, and electronics with some avant garde artists, including Robert Rauschenberg and John Cage, for the purpose of helping artists gain command of the astonishing new resources of sound and light that science makes available. As the artists gain from the technicians' help in solving creative problems in new media, the technicians gain from acquaintance with the aims and ways of art.

With nearly unimaginable consequences, the computer now is being made the servant of art, both as tool and as medium. Music has been composed by computer and in many diverse ways the computer is doing the mechanical and clerical work of the world now. Advertisements tell of computer "talking" to computer, library science centers on information retrieval by computer, and on every hand the work of the computer is becoming evident. But these for the most part are routine, noncreative uses of the machine, as when engineers program computers to determine the most efficient or economical or safest way to execute a construction project. Computers also serve the humanist in similar clerical and investigative ways.

Now, however, the computer can be used by the creative artist to aid him not in execution, although this can be done too, but in conception.* As the biophysicist can construct the image of a molecule on a screen and instruct the computer to modify it, rotate it, remember it, multiply it, and erase it, so

*Leslie Mezer "The Electronic Computer: a New Tool for the Artist" *Arts Canada* Feb. 1967. Issue No. 105, p. 20–21.

the sculptor can see the computer's image of his imagined form, can modify it, turn it around for study, record it, and recover it later. The act of imagination done incompletely and often lost through tricks of memory, now can be remembered and reproduced by machine. The sketchbook page with a dozen studies of a subject can be replaced by far more complete and varied visual data. And it is possible, when the sculptor is satisfied with his visualized model, for the machine to guide the tools that execute the work in wood or stone or metal. With color on the screen it is conceivable that the painter will adapt his art to the computer as his medium, with a whole new class of computer-generated and projected images. Furthermore, however tenuous and non-material as such a projected image may seem, translated into digital code it becomes more permanent than any paint or print or film yet made.

The main point, however, is that the computer so used becomes the clay and the modeling tool of the sculptor, and the palette and brush of the painter. For some time architects have been using computers to produce and develop their plans.

The implications are immense. The point of view implied by the terms humanities and humane now extends far beyond the polite scope of arts and letters, embracing culture in its widest sense. The arts seem destined to establish more and more connections between the disciplines of art and science. The study of the humanities, delving into the several arts to discover their likenesses and their unique qualities should lead to greater understanding of creative processes, and find in their typical combination of the humble and divine some true insight into the condition of being human.

▲   ▲   ▲

PLANNING THE HUMANITIES
SURVEY COURSE

KATHERINE HARBISON BOWERS

IN CONSIDERING how to present to you the problems inherent in planning a survey course in the Humanities, I have been reminded of a story current some years ago about an international essay contest on the subject of the elephant. Predictably, the French essay was entitled "L'Elephant et Ses Amours". The Germans sent in no mere essay, but a four-volume *Introduction to the Study of the Elephant,* with impressive bibliography and footnotes. The British essay was called "How I Killed an Elephant". This discussion is likely to be all too British—if indeed that *is* British—in its point of view. It has the advantage, however, of leaving plenty of room for you to write the American essay: "Bigger and Better Elephants".

I assume that you will wish to know several things: (1) which of several possible disciplines one might include in such a course; (2) in what sort of order these disciplines might be presented; (3) what specific materials one might wish to use; (4) what kinds of unifying correlations among the disciplines it may be possible to make; and (5) what kinds of equipment are necessary. Under the last heading, I shall touch briefly on probable administrative attitudes toward the required budget.

My responsible experience in such matters began in the fall of 1961 when I was appointed to teach something called Humanities at a brand new junior college to be run by the YMCA in Chicago's Loop. I was presented with an impresive catalog written by a group of bright young men strongly influenced by University of Chicago training. Its offerings included various survey courses at the 101-102 level. The description of the Humanities survey, however, was sufficiently vague to leave its actual organization in the hands of its first teacher.

In considering which of the five possible disciplines—history, philosophy, art, music, literature—should be included in such a survey, I eliminated history and philosophy for specific reasons. First, the teaching of history was already firmly in the hands of the social scientists. A better reason, however, for dismissing history was my firm belief that an actual experience of music, literature, and the visual arts may frequently be neutralized by too much initial inclusion of history. Essentially, all our education is so verbally oriented that we find it much too easy to read all about a work of art or music, for example, without ever really hearing or seeing the work itself. I certainly do not intend to imply that history and biography are not two authentic aspects of any work of art, but the work should, I feel, first speak for itself if one's approach is to be genuinely humanistic.

Second, philosophy was eliminated from the survey course—though not, of course, from the college curriculum—because of considerations of time and of teacher competence. Finding teachers willing to cope with three disciplines, I later discovered, is difficult enough. To add a fourth was tempting fate. This decision has since been reinforced by discussions with teachers in the city junior colleges where philosophy is included in the Humanities survey. Several of them expressed the opinion that such a work as the *Crito*, for example, ends by being taught purely as literature, and not as philosophy at all.

There remained, therefore, a curriculum of literature, music, and the visual arts to be organized with a sense of their common elements in such a way as to cover two semesters of fifteen weeks each before examination.

Aims and goals needed to be formulated. There was, first, a lofty one. By the end of two semesters, the student should be able to read any poem, story, or drama, to look at any example of the visual arts, to listen to any piece of music, with some degree of intelligence and understanding. Implicit in this goal was a second one—the development of the critical sense. "Critical" was a word I found it necessary to discuss with the students. It had to be made clear that criticism was not a matter of "It's good" or "It's bad," or "I like it" or "I don't like it;" that it involved considerable analysis of details that should not obscure the whole picture; that its aim was to discover what commentary a given work intended to make about the condition of mankind and how it was trying to do it.

Close to these aims was the desire to acquaint the students with the many resources of the city of Chicago, to make them aware of their great architectural heritage in the works of Louis Sullivan, and of Frank Lloyd Wright; to send our culturally improverished young people to find their own Opera House and Orchestra Hall and Art Institute. The first time I assigned a paper in Humanities 102 requiring the students to attend a live concert, I realized how important was that more pragmatic goal. "I had no idea so many people went to concerts," several of them wrote. "I think this should be required of every student."

The organization of the course the first year left much to be desired. The three disciplines were taught in blocks—ten weeks of literature in the first semester, followed by five of music; five of music in the second semester, followed by ten of the visual arts. The many connections among the arts were impossible to make clear in this manner, so the second year the course was reorganized. At first, the new approach seemed spotty and disconnected. Two weeks each of poetry, music and the visual arts, plus another fortnight of narrative fiction took us to midterm; then there were two more weeks each of music and visual arts, another week of poetry, and a final two weeks of music to finish the semester. But by examination time, there came to be a sense of unity and correlation in Humanities 101, and the system has been continued ever since. In Humanities 102, the semester began with further general study of the arts, with more attention to the visual arts this time, and with drama the focus of literature. In the latter half of the semester, biography and history began to be incorporated to some extent. One outstanding exponent of each of the arts was chosen for concentrated, if all too brief, attention. It was decided the three should be contemporary with each other. Recent choices have been Kandinsky, Stravinsky, and Dylan Thomas, who are obviously more or less contemporary with ourselves.

As the the the precise materials to be used in each section of a Humanities survey, let me say at once that I do not recommend any available textbooks. You have a golden opportunity here to write your own, beginning, perhaps, with an increasingly comprehensive syllabus. Our first three texts were the ones used by the University of Chicago. Their titles, at least, indicated our intentions—*Learning to Listen*,[1] *Learning to Look*,[2] and *What Happens in Literature*.[3] Professor Rosenheim, the author of the book on literature, says in his introduction that he wanted to make the title parallel with the others and call it *Learning to Read*, but feared he might be misunderstood. There are many students for whom the latter title would be highly appropriate. We are still using *Learning to Look*, but somewhat against the will of those of us who are not specialists in the visual arts.

I have been requested to concentrate on the materials of music. In this area, the big question is always: what can the student actually hear?

There are, of course, many ways of listening to music as all the music appreciation books agree. In our time, it is necessary to stress the difference between hearing and listening. Contemporary man is so bombarded with sound of all sorts that he would be quite mad if he listened to all he hears. To many of my students the idea of concentrated listening is strange and outlandish. Music is something to add excitement to a conversation that it almost drowns out. Or it is something to dance to— naturally—or to keep one from feeling lonesome while one is doing one's homework, or to provide a background for one's daydreams. The legitimacy of any or all of these uses for music is beside the point. The teacher can only hope to be correct in saying to the student that what is being offered in the music section of a Humanities survey will add a valuable dimension to his experience of music, and, like other aspects of the Humanities, increase his pleasures and his understanding of life.

---

[1]Cooper, G. *Learning to Listen*. University of Chicago Press.
[2]Taylor, J. C. *Learning to Look*. University of Chicago Press.
[3]Rosenheim, E. W. *What Happens in Literature*. University of Chicago Press.

One begins, of course, with the fundamentals of music—rhythm, melody, harmony, and tone color, with texture close behind them. The order in which one will decide to present these fundamentals depends on the point of view. Until recently, I have begun with rhythm, discussing meter first. For the less musical student, it has seemed advisable to reduce meter simply to duple and triple. Four-four time then becomes a form of duple meter. It is often hard to explain to people without musical training how they can hear the compound meters—6/8, 9/8, 12/8—but it can be done. What you will wish to do with the Eastern European quintuple and septuple meters will depend on your class and the time at your disposal. To the extent that you use contemporary composers, you may wish to show how in the midst of their irregularities, they interpose sections of regular meters from time to time—oases, no doubt, for the performer. In any case, you will, of course, draw attention to accented and unaccented beats. You may attend to such minutiae as whether the melody begins on an upbeat or a downbeat, the success of student recognition depending frequently on the clarity of the performance your recording or your live musician offers them.

The concept of rhythm as opposed to meter, or as including meter may be more difficult. The complicated rhythms of jazz improvisors over the regularity of the jazz beat may help to make this clear. For harmonic rhythms, the preludes in the "Well-Tempered Clavier" are frequently useful.

Then what can one teach about that most subtle musical element called melody? To learn to remember melodies, to give them immediate aural recognition, is a *sine qua non* for the understanding of the many homophonic structures, and some of the polyphonic ones as well. Two elements that are teachable are movement and contour. It is often possible for the student to recognize whether the melody moves in step-wise (conjunct) motion—like "My Country 'Tis of Thee"—or in chord outlines (disjunct motion)—like "The Star-Spanlged Banner". Then there is the shape of a melody. Leon Dallin's *Listener's Guide to Musical Understanding* has some interesting suggestions for

105

drawing diagrams of melodic contours.

For most students, harmony remains largely in the verbal realm. One can illustrate triads, seventh chords, and the more complicated ones like thirteenths, etc., whose notes may be sharped and flatted until one is involved in polytonality—or in atonality, if there is such a thing. One can try to explain consonance and dissonance, not in terms of pleasantness or unpleasantness, but of tension and relaxation. Here a touch of history may be pertinent. The chances are that none of your pupils will be even slightly shocked at the sound of an unprepared dominant seventh chord. Yet when Monteverdi first used one in 1600, diatribes were written against the dreadful sounds he was making. Some of the dissonances that sound so extreme to us today may seem equally as tame to the next generation as Monteverdi's horrid dominant seventh does to us.

Then there is modality. I have never been able to teach the sound of major and minor to students without a musical background—never, that is, until this past semester. I have, so far, no idea what is the cause of my success or lack of it. I know only that now the majority of students can tell me correctly if a musical selection is principally major or minor, whereas formerly most of them could not. For the older modal scales there are, of course, plainsong and many of the American folksongs of British origin. I like to call attention to the dramatic effect on the folk poetry of the unflatted sixth in the Dorian mode, as illustrated by one of the Appalachian versions of "John Riley". The chromatic scale will lead you to Wagner, for instance, and perhaps eventually to show how in contemporary music, it has completely destroyed the whole concept of major and minor.

Tone color is an excuse for teaching recognition of different types and registers of the human voice as well as instruments of the orchestra and the various keyboard instruments. This is probably the place, also to discuss mediums—orchestras and bands, choral and madrigal groups, string quartets, woodwind ensembles, and so forth. For many classes, beginning with this element is more appealing than becoming at once involved with the more mathematical aspects of music.

The homophonic structures are the next natural step. For binary forms there are movements from Baroque keyboard suites; for ternary, popular songs and Mozart minuets. There are themes and variations, of course, and rondos, and finally the complications of sonata-allegro form. I tend to lean on Mozart for many of these since he is so obligingly clear. For polyphonic forms, such as the fugue, I have not hesitated to use the Bach performances of the Swingle Singers, but only after the class has thoroughly examined the original versions.

But all this must sound like a superficial course in music appreciation, so let us move to a consideration of the many correlations between the arts. To begin with one's own natural vocabulary is enlightening. Already you are using some of the same words both literally and metaphorically. Line, for example, belongs to painting. Yet melody is often said to describe a line or curve that may be smooth or jagged. Homophonic music has one primarily horizontal line above a series of harmonic verticals. Polyphonic music is a group of horizontal lines with verticals largely implied. Poetry has lines whose character may, again, be rough or smooth, abruptly ending with a masculine accent, or tapering gracefully away with an unaccented feminine curve. We speak of a "story line" and of lines of development in plot and character.

Tone belongs to music. Yet we speak of tone in literature as indicating where the author's sympathies lie, and we say that painters have tone, or don't have it; that they paint in low or high keys. Examples of rhythm in architecture and prose as well as music and poetry are multitudinous. Movement is equally inseparable from them all.

Texture belongs to material things in and out of the visual arts. Yet we have spoken of musical texture, and few or many lines in a plot may make its texture transparent or dense.

Colorful orchestration and colorful characters and settings, though metaphorical, are effective in much the same way as the literally vivid colors of a Matisse or a Bonnard. Equally widespread is chiaroscuro. Tschaikovsky's Sixth Symphony begins and ends in darkness, with the relief of lightness especially in the second movement. Such a poem as Robert Frost's "Come In" is a study in dark and light, as is Hawthorne's short story, "Young Goodman Brown."

"Thus inadvertently," says Curt Sachs in *The Commonwealth of Art*, "we often speak of what is dormant deep in our consciousness: that the basic forces at the bottom of art do not change whether we build, carve, paint, or compose."

One small warning about the process of discovering these "basic forces". Be sure your analogies are authentic. For one example: the ABA structure exists in both architecture and music, but let us draw our parallels with care. The facade of a Gothic cathedral is more like a musical ABA than its nave and transepts. In music, it is the A's that are important. Thus the spires and the rose window give the importance to A, whereas in the cathedral's interior, the nave, corresponding to the B section, has more importance than the A transepts. It is consequently less like the ternary musical form, and more like the musical "arch" form, as in the third movement of Hindemith's "Mathis der Maler".

The most difficult part of this teaching, it has seemed to me, is to make clear to immature students the way in which these common elements not only produce individual works of art, but say something as well about the condition of man. Perhaps I can best illustrate how this can be done by considering the three contemporary artists chosen for the end of the course. Kandinsky, Stravinsky, and Thomas must all show us somehow the state of contemporary man. The question is: How?

We may safely agree, I hope, that man, as the center of the universe, is in almost as precarious a condition as was the earth as a similar center once Galileo had used his telescope. Is this what is reflected in Kandinsky's abandonment of man and his familiar environment as subject matter for his paintings? He is not even interested, it seems, in the effect of lights on familiar objects as were his Impressionist predecessors. Apparently inchoate strivings, which are bound to offend conventional

108

minds, characterize his middle period. His final solutions involve either geometric patterns or shapes resembling primitive life forms. Is this not at least a reflection on the general shake-up in values of our day?

Stravinsky's predecessors developed their themes, suggesting the possibility of evolution in character and circumstances. Stravinsky tends to make few changes in his themes except to use different instruments for their announcement—the same characters appear simply in new clothes. As he adopts the twelve-tone method of composition, they turn backward or upside-down, they take a longer or a shorter time to present themselves, but change by growth appears not to be a part of their experience. Such change as occurs is governed by strictly mathematical laws. Movement is spiral. The same experiences take place in different guises.

Examples from the poetry of Dylan Thomas could be inexhaustible. To mention two: puny man does not look upward at the towering flames after a fire raid; rather, Thomas speaks of "the fire-dwarfed street;" and the evanescence of man is described in one of his alterations in a familiar phrase—not once *upon* a time, but once *below* a time, below the time when man appeared from—where?

The ambiguities of the twentieth century are likewise represented in the work of all three. Kandinsky makes us uncertain about what is in front of what or on top of what. We cannot be sure in which directions objects point or of whether his movement is meant to be clockwise or counter-clockwise; either approach is equally logical, and everything really happens at once. Stravinsky confuses us with more than one tonality. Should we, perhaps, be encouraged by the fact that he insists on a clear underlying tonality in his tone-row music as Schoenberg and his followers did not?

And there are other reasons for encouragement. All three men are deeply conscious of the overlap of the arts. Kandinsky bases his abstractions on the idea, specifically expressed in his writings, that painting must be more like music if it is to be true to itself. Thomas writes "a play for voices"; he writes poems shaped to look visually like wombs or chalices. Stravinsky adopts the structural proportions of Venice's St. Mark's for the sections of his "Canticum Sacrum."

The work of others, past and present, in the same art affects each of them profoundly. Kandinsky's abstract ideas began with his reactions to Monet's "Haystacks". It is easy to discover in the work of Thomas the influences of Vaughan, Housman, Marvell, Hopkins, and the Book of Genesis. Stravinsky began his work with Diaghilev by orchestrating Chopin for ballet music. His Pulcinella suite is based on the work of Pergolesi; his opera, "The Rake's Progress", uses Mozartean recitatives with characteristically sparse harpsichord accompaniment.

Have we the right to conclude from this that in spite of disturbances, there is still a comforting continuity?

The process of turning from these fascinating speculations to the securing of the necessary equipment for presenting our courses is often a painful descent. Ideally, there should be a Humanities room with a stationary record player, protected by lock and key from even unintentional abuse. Screens should be permanently installed, as should slide projectors. It might even be possible to persuade your librarian somehow to keep the school's collection of recordings and slides in the same room. How often does a question from a class lead a teacher legitimately off to the use of illustrations not previously planned! How wonderful if the examples were readily available in the middle of a class period!

Perhaps most important to the teaching of music for the purposes of the Humanities are adequate listening rooms for students. Listening assignments should be part of the normal homework—perhaps supervised, perhaps not, depending on circumstances. Simply reading about music is totally inadequate preparation.

Yet you may well find your administrators startled by the idea of equipment for Humanities courses. At the beginning, it was with great difficulty that we were able to secure for our college a collection of art slides. When money was provided for their purchase, there was not enough to buy them already framed. The library staff had to put them in their frames after they arrived. Even so, some administrators seemed continually surprised to find they were actually being used. Now in our sixth year, we are finally likely to have an adequate record library, for we are in the process of accreditation, and equipment is necessary if we are to be accredited. We were to have had proper rooms for listening assignments, but just as they were about to be prepared, somebody upstairs decided to rent that floor of the building to a business firm for its offices. There are administrators who still regard it as peculiar that the Humanities survey should be part of the required curriculum. Humanities, they seem to think, are a frill. One can afford to become interested in the arts after he has established himself economically.

For this is the day of the scientist who will have comparatively little trouble securing all the laboratory equipment he needs. This, of course, we don't begrudge him. It is the inequities that jar one. For the method of the scientist is rightly to limit and narrow the problem at hand so as to fit it into a design that permits controlled testing and quantification. The method of the humanist involves the recognition that life experience cannot be so narrowed. It is the unexpected entrance of new elements, the unforeseen result of an action or a character trait with which we must learn to deal. It is not our business to solve problems, but to learn how to live with them, how to balance our tiny umbrellas of philosophic knowledge as we walk the thin, vibrant tight-rope of life in these and all other ambiguous times.

The scientist from the Argonne laboratories who recently said to me that, of course, a man could not consider himself educated if he was not well versed in the Humanities was expressing not a new idea, but an important one. Somewhat more novel was the statement of a young man doing research at Cape Kennedy.

111

"In a few years," he said anxiously, "only about twenty percent of the labor force will be necessary to run the machines. And what will the rest do? For them the Humanities will be a necessity."

He was thinking, I suppose, of all those enormous amounts of leisure time. I hope he did not ignore the contribution of humanistic studies to the problem of learning to live with ourselves in new and unprecedented situations.

In any case, even if his prognosis is not completely accurate, I believe we should remember it as we plan those bigger and better Humanities courses.

References consulted or cited:

Dallin, Leon: *Listener's Guide to Musical Understand,* Dubuque, Wm. C. Brown Co., 1965

Olson, Elder: *The Poetry of Dylan Thomas,* Chicago, University of Chicago Press, Phoenix Edition, 1961

Sachs, Curt: *The Commonwealth of Art,* N. Y., Norton, 1946

Varg, Paul A.: "The Proposed Foundation for the Humanities", *The Journal of Higher Education,* Ohio State University Press, Vol. XXXVI, No. 5, May 1965

THE following section has been extracted from an open discussion held at the conclusion of the conference.

Comments and questions otherwise unidentified are those of the audience.

Q. Do you have any comments on the evaluation of attempts to present an appreciative aspect of art?

Bowers: I have found it advisable, particularly in the realm of music and in the visual arts, to try to persuade my students to cultivate objectivity rather than any emotional appreciation for the simple reason that mine come so filled with prejudices. "There's no music but jazz." "If I can't recognize what the picture is about immediately, then it's no good," etc. For that reason I have found it wise in these first two semesters simply to cultivate objectivity and say, "What is in it? What do you hear? What do you see?" The appreciation does come incidentally.

Apropos of how do you know what you've done, a study of fatigue in different occupations showed the teacher was the most subject to fatigue for the simple reason that his or her rewards don't come when the work is done, and so you go home not knowing whether you have any rewards. A young man in one of my classes, seemingly a total clod, made a D or an F. Six months later I ran into him in the hall and he said, "You know, Mrs. Bowers, I keep my poetry book by my bed and read it every night before I go to sleep." All I can say is, something had happened!

Q. If you had a class which knew the fundamentals, would you approach music differently?

Bowers: Somewhat, yes. I might include more history and biography but I still would not allow that to be the main emphasis. I would use an approach something like Aaron Copland in "What to Listen for in Music" and Machlus in "Enjoyment of Music."

Q. What kind of an answer do you expect when you ask a student "What do you hear?"

Bowers: I would not ask any question so general as that. My experience is that there is nothing that any student likes better than to tell you what daydreams are suggested to him. I would say, "What instruments do you hear?" "How many melodies do you hear?" being very specific about certain aspects of music.

Q. The main speakers have talked about music, art, poetry, and literature and did not talk too much about philosophy and religion in the humanities. Is this being stressed less?

Bowers: It depends upon your primary institution and upon the relation of the course to the rest of the curriculum. It was not my intention to neglect either philosophy or religion in planning the course. I did this for practical reasons. We had a good philosophy department, and it is even better now than it was before; also we have such a variety of religious beliefs in this group, from Bahai to Judaism to any number of different Christian divisions. It seemed wiser not to include religion as such, but religious questions do inevitably come up in discussing literature, in presenting pictures, in whatever you do. You cannot avoid them and you don't try to. But how much they are stressed depends upon the institution.

Chairman: To inject an editorial comment here, it's also very difficult to find people who'll feel competent in dealing with these topics in secondary or even community college context. This is a thing that frightens a good many people and they usually wish it off unto specialists at the higher levels.

Q. How can we integrate our civilized structure to make it more meaningful? Where is it going with us and where are we going with it?

Comment: In the humanities what we are faced with are really value questions. This might be the reason why certain areas of science might be opposed to the humanities in that in the sciences you wouldn't be allowed to have an open-ended question such as the one just presented; whereas, in the humanities you are confronted with open-ended questions. For example, where we are with our own society? how we came this way? which direction are we going? The humanities would allow us, then, to have as many different answers as there would be individuals in the room. Such questions as these would probably not be raised in the science situation.

Chairman: Isn't science basically involved in a descriptive task which puts it in a slightly different realm, gives it a slightly different concern?

Comment: In the humanities you have to evaluate a thing that cannot be measured objectively. I don't think science is opposed to the humanities. Let us say man started out as a pure animal. If he had some scientific problems to solve, like survival, he invented tools. We've still got the same problem as far as that's concerned. Now our tools are a little more intricate, but we have another problem coming up; that is, to not go with the solutions. In other words, not just be a scientific being and leave the fact that we are human. I don't think we will be able to do that very successfully, but it could mean our destruction if we go too far without being human.

Chairman: That's very true. I remember a program not too long ago in which one of the men, who was involved with the chemical department in World War II, was trying to make this precise point as a biological scientist. The scientist since Enrico Fermi and his group's successful experiment in the squash courts of the University of Chicago can no longer avoid the value judgment as we can. We must look at the implications of what the science and the technology are doing. I think this is also one of the reasons we are getting much more of a play on the humanities today—it is finally beginning to dawn on us that we have a moral responsibility for what science is creating and we had better take a long, hard look at it.

Comment: Then we have come to a full circle in the humanities. There is no discipline or subject area that can be divorced from a humanitarian or, better yet, humanistic approach. The definition of humanities becomes "where you can teach the humanities." There would be no area that was not included. You would have to use this approach no matter what subject area you are in.

Comment: There are humanistic questions in any subject area if we accept as a basic concern and tentative definition of the humanities the fact that we must look at what makes us

116

human, look at the human values that we have and evaluate them in terms of our present situation. Can we limit this to art, music, literature, philosophy, drama, or must this also extend into all the other domains to some extent? May there not be a humanistic approach to science? There was once, Dr. Matthews pointed out last Saturday.

Q. I would like to raise the question of adults judging what children's needs are. As human beings children's needs basically are for survival. They're in conflict with our headlines, with our radio and TV showing. How do we judge their needs for survival? In what way are we going to nourish their instinctive drives toward love and affection and brotherhood, etc., which I believe are basic with children?

Comment: She's covered what has been talked about by Dr. De Mott. It hasn't been solved; it's got to have a solution somewhere. Humanism and Science are face to face with each other, but they've got to integrate in order for us to continue. She's expressing, in my opinion, exactly the same thing. Yes, we could give these children in elementary school a talk or two on all those things that have to do with survival and brotherhood the week before they were to start the scientific learning, using discovery or whatever technique desired. But what right do we have to decide that this group of children is now ready and *human* enough to go on and start learning scientific things?

Comment: We are unnecessarily drawing lines between the sciences and the arts. I think this is a consequence of the human mind and it's getting in our way of solving these problems. Going back to an earlier statement, these problems are all interrelated and the things that we teach should have a humanistic approach.

Q. What are the implications of this now for the way in which we structure our programs in our schools? Most schools have some kind of subject departments and this in college, as well as in secondary and to some extent in elementary schools, tends to reinforce the separation. As educators is there anything that we can do to make sure that we are going to somehow integrate these experiences?

A. It would seem to me that one way to start doing this would be for teachers not necessarily to have a team-teaching situation, but at least a team-planning situation, where the teachers themselves—through an exchange of ideas within a particular building—would be able to separate themselves from their content area to the extent that they are going to be stating exactly what objectives they hope to accomplish in their course as far as this student is involved. Then as each teacher would do that in their particular subject matter area or content area, it would be interesting to see if a common denominator would appear in such terms as "I would like my student to be able to think; I would like him to see the relationships between . . ." This might possibly break down the dynasty of coordinators, the dynasty of departments within buildings and bring about a true integration and humanistic approach, focusing the attention not on the subject matter but on learning.

Comment: I just want to reinforce what this chap said. However, I think the danger lies in the fact that we are all afraid to lose our identity, especially in our areas, and I'll speak for music myself. I know this has come up in a team teaching situation. As a matter of fact the youngsters who are getting music in the team teaching situation are getting a much broader and a much better class than the general, regular music prescribed class. Youngsters who are getting music in team teaching must take it regardless. Some teachers are afraid of losing identity because they would be swimming with the rest rather than alone. People must begin to see that we're out to educate the whole child, not to give a smattering of this and a smattering of that and a smattering of the other. If we keep this objective in mind, I think we can accomplish some of these goals.

Comment: I'd like to underscore that also. If you are going to have planning sessions together, it's got to be very regular, every day and ample time for different discipline people to get together. The result is not that you lose your identity as, for example, a music humanities teacher or an art humanities teacher. It is that you're able to put your energy into the program and that is the important thing. An English teacher's idea of fine arts humanities would probably be Romantic program music and Romantic painting depicting very emotional things. It takes the identity of a strong art person or a strong music person to work in a group.

Chairman: This is a very sensitive area, and one that causes very real anxieties on the part of administrators and teachers. Are you now involved in a team situation?

A. Yes, and instead of losing my identity as a musician, I have increased and enlarged my identity in a very rewarding way.

Comment: I have the same problem with teacher training students in other areas. The institution today is not humanistic. It is not geared for a person.

Q. How do we get the message to the teacher training institutions? Do we make our little placards and go march? Is there some way we can make this felt?

A. That certainly is a place to start, but too often—as in statements we have just heard—the notion is that a person has completed his education when he leaves the teacher training institution. In my judgment this is only the beginning. Maybe what they're doing in teacher training institutions is adequate in some ways, but when a person leaves a teacher training institution he should have learned that he can go out and develop and mature on his own. If they have failed in any way, it is in this way that they've failed. They haven't given this message loudly and clearly to their graduates.

Chairman: I can't help but interject an old favorite story of mine. A number of years ago a man finally left Harvard at the age of seventy, having taken most of the courses he could get himself into, and as a valedictory remark said, "Now I am ready to face the world." I think the concept of continuing education is certainly one that we are increasingly aware of. One advantage—and I think that this is implicit if not explicit

119

in several of the observations here—that a team situation can offer is a growth experience. If you have to defend the wanting to include a more Romantic approach to art and music in a team situation and your contemporary minded art colleague can't stand the Romantic schools, this is going to cause, hopefully at least, a creative interplay and perhaps each of you might modify and be a little the more for it. The interesting thing is that in reading the research on team teaching that has been done, what happens to the students apparently is not as great as we had hoped for in the beginning. We thought that this was going to do an awful lot for the students. Well, it doesn't really. What it does do, it does an awful lot for the teachers. When the school sets up a creative situation for team teaching and is really committed to it and not following an educational fad (which is a problem we have, let's face it), the teachers who are involved in this quite often find that they are having a heck of a lot of fun. Obviously if the teachers are enjoying what they are doing, there's going to be a certain amount of spill-over for the students. Although in terms of whatever testing and periodical evaluation we have been able to do there's not a great deal of direct fallout to the student, the team teaching approach has done wonders for the teachers! If this is the result that we get, this alone is sufficient grounds for exploring the team approach.

Q. The problem of Time. We all have pretty full schedules. When are we going to get time to sit down with colleagues and plan, and explore, and just think? Are any schools represented here that have found good techniques for getting time set aside?

A. I think that's going to have to be worked on from the angle of the board of education and building principals—administrators in general. They must realize that time must be put into the program. We have a humanities-geography combination in our building. We do have a common planning time for art and music people with the other teachers. These music and art teachers can get to the classroom. There is some time available, maybe not as much as we'd like.

In other buildings in our system the scheduling (which could have been done by a principal who just re-arranged his schedule or who had convinced the board of his need for more personnel) wasn't done. In these buildings the program is on the shoulders of one individual who had to become an expert in all fields, quite a difficult thing to do. It can be done. You have to cut down on the number of classes; you may have to hire more teachers. This is something an individual teacher cannot control, but administrators and boards have come to realize that if you want team teaching you have to have the planning time.

Q. Doesn't team teaching relieve some of the scheduling problems? If you were working as an individual teacher, at times you might have to take some extra classes. I thought one of the benefits of a team teaching situation was that one teacher would take a larger group, relieving the other teacher for further preparation, etc.

Chairman: This certainly was one of the benefits that Lloyd Trump envisioned for team teaching. Is it working out that way? How about some of the people who are involved in it?

A. In the one situation I know about personally, we found that the rapport or relationship between the various teachers didn't work unless we were all present. Since there were more people involved for one period, it cost the school more money.

Q. Did the school find objection to this or were they willing to pay?

A. They were willing.

Comment: We have a number of teams in our school. Teams are given one period a week of about 45 minutes. This isn't very much time and the period really gets eroded because we do have other commitments. We do manage to plan a week ahead at this time in a general way, but to really plan in any detail we have to meet after school. We set a general direction and members of the team talk over their own approach to whatever theme we have decided upon, very beneficial. We're not working as five individuals; we're working as a team despite the fact that we have only 45 minutes. Then we are all together on the large book meetings when the lectures are given so that we will go along as a team on a major subject, each of us developing it in our own small groups. This probably isn't very ideal, but it is the team approach.

Comment: I teach in a school outside Grand Rapids where Humanities Program 317 is excellent. There are six people involved in the team situation. Actually we're only in the classroom four hours out of a six hour day—the first hour of each day is our team meeting and the hour after lunch is conference time. The schedule was set up so that we'd have plenty of time to discuss. Extra-curricular activities come before and after school, beyond the call of duty!

Q. What takes place at one of these team meetings? What type of discussion goes on?

A. A multitude of things. If introducing a piece of literature to correlate with an historical period, the English people involved will talk. The different approaches to be used we discuss thoroughly, trying to come to some conclusion. When we're testing, the person or persons who made out the test read the test aloud so that every teacher knows what's going to be tested. Thus, if we have to make a last minute coverage on some point, we have an opportunity.

Q. I have some reservations about approaching the problem as presented this morning by Professor De Mott, administrative reservations. When I hear this gentleman speaking about getting together to make sure the test questions are all lined up properly, I wonder if that fits in with your definition of the humanistic approach.

A. I think the catch there is that we still are required to mark report cards. Our administrators and boards require some form of evaluation sent home. Whether you like to or not you are requested to appraise, or evaluate, or quiz the performance—use whatever word you want. A test carefully planned among a group of teachers would be much more effective than two standardized tests which don't attempt to evaluate different groups of children.

Comment: We readily recognize this problem and we as a team often remark that actually what we're doing is just teaching for a test. Once again we are back in the old problem of evaluation, our hands are tied, and we haven't solved the problem.

Q. Are we talking about the elementary school or the secondary school?

A. I would suspect that we're primarily concerned about secondary school at the moment, but would not some of the same problems also apply at the elementary level?

Comment: Professor De Mott said perhaps his most meaningful time was during the planning of a class; the most human time, a group interchange or gossip. That's when ideas come out. It's irrelevant, really, whether you're forming a test or what you're doing. The conversation that goes on between the teachers, the dialogue, is the important thing.

Comment: Is this also losing identity and accepting the humanities approach and the humanities philosophy? If there is still fear, is not this proof that the new approach has not yet been accepted?

Q. Dr. Matthews, when he talked about the humanities in our changing world, mentioned anthropology and culture with a capital "C" versus the small "c" culture of the deculture. Would Mrs. Bowers comment on this?

Bowers: The whole field of epic musicology is one that will speak to the students in a very real way and can be used as a springboard. I try to include different kinds of music in my classes and one day I played a jazz record one of the boys had brought in. I couldn't get the class to go. The period went by and all the "flying objects" were as relaxed as could be. I made up my mind then that I'm going to work out a music appreciation course that stems from jazz, but it's going to take me awhile because I don't know enough to do it!

Comment: The elementary teachers have a golden opportunity that the high school teachers don't have, tied as they are to a one hour block of time in one subject. The elementary school teacher has been tying herself down too, and unnecessarily. It used to be that the teacher had to cover a particular textbook, but the multi-text and multi-material (even at the elemenary level) frees the teacher. She can choose her own ways to teach the basic skills, the ways to which she finds her own class responds.

We taught humanities to the second grade and took these second graders to the art museum. They got more out of it than many juniors and seniors with no background. Young children can take a lot more than people realize. They take it home and talk to their parents about it. Ask them what they're studying and they don't say the new math; they say they're studying primitive society and can tell you about it.

Chairman: At Brookside School Cranbrook they have set up a block of time which is available for a cross-disciplinary approach. The teachers can then exercise their own interests and competency a little more freely. In one grade they take as their theme the book *The Quiet Crisis*[*] by Secretary of the Interior Udal. In their social studies, in their science and in their English they use this as the broad theme for the year. You can imagine where you can go from this. If you take a look at the general theme of conservation and science, conservation of human resources in terms of social sciences, you get involved in ecology. You can take off and go in a variety of areas. The children understand this and it presents them with a vehicle by which they can grasp the inter-relationships of what's going on in their science class with what's going on in their social science class. They see man as a social being also interacting with the world of nature around him, concerned with the implications of what science has to say in terms of how we can make good use of the land around us. We can see how exceedingly fruitful this approach is where it is being tried on the elementary level. There are more possibilities at the secondary level than we have been willing to look for heretofore.

---

[*]Udall, Stewart; *The Quiet Crisis*. Holt, Rinehart & Winston, New York.

Q. How would the humanist go about teaching two plus two equals four?

A. He wouldn't teach it unless there was a need for it.

Comment: Nevertheless, it seems that with the humanistic approach, the team teaching approach, the cross-disciplinary approach—however you want to describe this general one—there comes a point where a proficiency in a particular skill or subject matter, such as how much is two plus two, is very vital. A polarity comes about between your desire for integration on the part of the student, and the body of knowledge that you want the student to have as a result of ten months of a particular course. Also, handling a subject on such a broad theme basis exposes a teacher in front of the class—his proficiencies and his weaknesses. What's one's immediate reaction to that!

Comment: This is the basic problem of trying to find some breadth as well as depth in an area. What are the minimum basic skills that a student should have? What are his basic proficiencies? How much does he need to know? For example, in teaching music how much of the language of music does he need to know? How much of the techniques does he need to know? Once we have come through this particular discipline it's awfully easy for us to want to give them more than they really need; yet, on the other hand, we've got to make sure they do get the fundamentals, whatever is basic. I don't know how many of you have tried to sit down in your own area and say what are the basic minimums the student must have in order to survive, in order to get long in this area. How much of what we tend to do, and often enjoy doing because it is meaningful to us, do we include that we could really omit?

Q. Professor De Mott this morning did a beautiful job on his idea of helping a student articulate his own consciousness, but if we really want to appreciate a poem as a work of art don't we have to see the structure, the juxtaposing of images, the economy of expression, etc.? I think the professor condescends to this in his own teaching. I don't think that any student can go away and pick up a poetry book and love it because

125

it's just a plot to help him articulate his own experience—existential. I wonder what the group thought about that. I don't think that you'll ever get a true appreciation of any art unless you get into the terms of that art.

Comment: I wonder how much of this goes into the mind of an artist, or a composer, or a poet when writing a work. Are they trying to communicate something in a formal style, or are they simply trying to bring across an idea which comes out in a certain style because of their training? We've been taught that certain styles are right for poetry, and little children who can't find a rhyme are sometimes very disappointed. I was wondering if this is something that's needed and something to be taught first or if style, as he suggests, should be examined only if it comes up. Can you enjoy a poem without understanding a rhyme scheme? Does it speak to you without a rhyme scheme? Does it speak to you without your knowing how it was constructed? Perhaps communication is what De Mott was talking about and not formal structure.

Comment: I would certainly say he was concerned primarily with the communication at this point and using the poem as a medium or vehicle or, as he put it, as a voice in a dialogue. I suspect he probably does some other things too, but this was the brunt of his argument.

Comment: I think you can go into enough detail to make the children detest poetry. You have to make a child want to enjoy poetry, not the reason a young man wrote it. The child has to enjoy the poem because of something in it. In any subject the children have to enjoy the thing they're reading.

Comment: You can't enjoy an art form, you know, unless you enjoy the art.

Comment: I think understanding and appreciating are two different things. I can appreciate a piece of music but have no idea whether it's major, minor or all those other terms that were used this morning. I appreciate it and can get a message from it, but this may not be the same message that Mozart or someone had in mind, but to me that's not important.

126

Bowers: What do you mean by appreciate?

Comment: I just like it and it says something to me.

Bowers: That's all right. Good. Go to it. On the other hand I still think it should say more to you.

Comment: I was the clod.

Bowers: No, I don't believe that!

Comment: I wish to back up Mrs. Bowers. I believe that the experience in music can be on two different levels. One might go and listen to a symphony and have one total experience that is totally satisfactory; but if one knows the score and has the score in one's lap and is following it, there is a different experience—each is total, each is valid in its own sphere. If you're thinking of education the first experiences are first concern, but the others certainly—if we're full human beings, intellectual beings—are something to be desired too; but I think they're both total.

Comment: Did you happen to watch Leonard Bernstein's "Young People's Concert" on television when his subject was the composer Ives? To me this was an example of what we're trying to say here. That music that we heard in the beginning! —I didn't know what to make of it. I didn't know where to put it. I didn't know whether to go out of the room and abandon it or just sit there and make believe I understood it. Then Bernstein told about the composer, explained the composition, and played the George Washington piece. It was so meaningful— you could put yourself into it and really enjoy the music and understand it from the point of view of the composer and what he was trying to do. But that happened only after the explanation. I probably would have gotten a limited appreciation if I listened to the piece but enjoyed it or not enjoyed it, I don't know. With the explanation, the understanding of what chords he was using, his philosophy, the piece came alive the way it should have come alive.

I think this whole business of the humanities is the business of broadening and trying to raise people above the immediate

127

dogmatic reaction. I had a recent experience with a student teacher that came to me from a school in which they taught a lot of this immediate gut reaction with no sense of form. The poor little thing couldn't teach because she had nothing *to* teach, because she absolutely knew nothing about what she was doing. She would hold up the students' work and all she could really say was, "Oh, I like this; it's so . . ." or "I don't like that," and put it down. Really, we're in the business of trying to raise us above this, "It's immediate to me; I like it." There's a lot more to it than that.

Comment: I think it's the same question that was asked over here: how do you teach one plus one is two? Someone answered that a humanist teacher doesn't give it to one who doesn't want to learn it. A humanist doesn't say he doesn't believe in planning. I think there has to be some form in any kind of education. It's always been my belief that art and science have to have some sort of combination. A scientist has to have a divergent way of looking at things or else he would never come across anything new, but he can't let that be the only way he looks. He must test, he must prove, he must be able to evaluate so that the combination of the art and science together make a full human being, a full approach to anything.

Comment: This problem about "I don't want to analyze it because I like it." How about the things you don't like? This is the big question. I remember the first time I heard "The Rite of Spring." I was very young and fresh out of a small town in central Kentucky—you can imagine how absolutely fascinating "Le Sacre du Printemps" was when I came to Boston knowing only hymns and Italian operatic arias! But now this is a marvelous piece of music to me. How did I get that way? By learning what Stravinsky is trying to do. One more thing—Leonard Bernstein's been mentioned. A lot of my earnest jazz hounds have learned to appreciate jazz better because of listening to Leonard Bernstein's record "What Is Jazz?"

Comment: If we really believe what we are saying about how important the humanities are and how vital it is that our boys and girls are taught with this approach, there is an urgency on the part of both teacher training institutions and public schools to try to involve *all* our teachers in experiences that would guide them in this kind of thinking. We should start thinking seriously about some "blanket" kind of knowledge.

Chairman: If we feel any conviction in this area we normally have to go back to our own schools and lobby, so to speak, for what we want. I think we also need to make sure that the schools, the colleges, the teacher training institutions get their feedback too. Either in form of letter or personal conversation these institutions need to know—and any of them that are worth their salt *want* to know—what our needs are and what our feelings are. Most of them would welcome an opportunity. So I would suggest that you go home and begin a letter writing campaign. This is going to have to be a multi-headed approach. We are going to have to jump on our horse and Don Quixote-like ride off in all directions at once and tackle it at the local school, through the various professional organizations, and—through communicating with the colleges so they are aware that we feel strongly. Often there is a real problem of how to get feedback. The colleges haven't solved the problem to knowing what it is that the teachers feel and what they need in their day-to-day experiences. If we're going to mount a significant effort, we can't wait for Washington to set up a new program for it. We're going to have to utilize every available channel whether it be to working with our colleagues over coffee and gossip, or participating in programs and institutes or letter writing. This is very important if we are going to make any really large scaled breakthroughs, and I think we can.

We may not have the pressures of the Sputnik that the scientists and mathematicians have, but we've got a more devastating pressure behind us when we look at the problems that our society is having in adjusting to all the tremendous changes that are going on. I don't think anybody here needs to be told that this is a time of tremendous change; and I think this has a great implications for what we do in the humanities—ranging from understanding and appreciating the value systems of others to what we're going to do with the leisure time that our society is going to have.

Comment: I wonder how many of us really thought how much the teaching of the humanities is a real threat to the establishment. You know, if we really believe in what we are doing, it's going to rub our poor shaky little world real hard. The establishment isn't going to like that. You know, also, teaching the humanities is kind of a teaching for peace, is a teaching of the worthwhileness of the individual, and I just don't mean the American individual. Can our society really stand the kind of things that we want to tell the children? They're getting wiser and they're going to start demanding some things. What happens when we try to teach creativity in the child's own identity and then he is told his hair can't be longer than his ears, that somehow his eyes are different from a girl's eyes and he can't see through his hair where a girl can? It seems kind of incongruous even in our little society, which is what the humanities really threatens. If you're really going to push the thing, you've got to expect some pretty severe criticism from the establishment.

Question: Is that the reason why it has to come from the bottom and not from the top? The reason that all valid learning has always been a kind of conspiracy?

Question: I'd like to inject another note into this discussion. I get concerned about people in the humanities and the arts always saying you must not mention emotion in any way. I wonder if in our attempt to be scientific and intellectual we're not making a mistake. It's all very well to say that in your evaluation of an art "I like" or "I don't like" is a personal thing, but then to throw out all emotion is to say that there must be no enthusiasm and no excitement. I don't believe this. I think we've got to keep the emotion.

Chairman: I don't think anybody has been advocating that we throw out emotion. I think the problem in many cases, as Mrs. Bowers said, is that the students made emotional judgments with no real basis for making them. In a sense you have to, for at least a period of time, neutralize the emotion so that you can provide some basis for a good emotional experience. Certainly if you go to see a Picasso show and feel nothing but simply analyze all his techniques, you've missed the boat. To truly appreciate Picasso you have to understand his techniques as well as have an emotional experience.

Comment: You can't keep emotion out; try and do it.

Chairman: The problem basically, as I said, is trying to get at the student who comes saying, "I don't like long-haired music" or "I don't like painting" or whatever, and simply has made a premature closure on the basis of what some of his contemporaries have said.

Comment: I had a student last year who somewhere along the line had decided that no painting was good except those done in the 17th century. When I put a slide on that wasn't from the 17th century he would tell me, "Now that's bad, you see, and this is the reason." Well, what can you do with somebody like that except to insist on another kind of objectivity? But you can't keep emotion out; it'll be there, don't worry.

Q. Don't you think that you have a much fuller and more satisfying emotional response to the picture after you understand it?

A. I think that's a generalization that just may not be so. It bothers me that we go from what we heard early this morning to this. Then so beautiful, I thought, *free* of some of the kinds of things that we are now talking about—body of knowledge, knowing the techniques. If that's going to be our expectations of the humanities, we're going to get trapped in the same thing that the mathematicians get trapped in and the scientists get trapped in: that you've got to know all the things before you can really be humane about it. That's the danger now although you may not have said exactly that. But it amazes me that we went from this beautiful thing early this morning to getting very technical this afternoon, and it shakes me up.

Comment: In line with what this man just said, we do have

a tendency to overintellectualize and we do seem still to be afraid of emotion. We, each of us, have a heart and a mind; they both need education, and I think that our job is to keep the two running parallel—if that's at all possible. We have been threatened in so many ways by the academic emphasis. We are in a new phrase of our evolution and aren't quite accustomed to this idea that we have to allow our emotions to keep up with our intellect.

The term was used earlier, so I can use one of my pet phrases and that's "concept bi-polarity." I think that this is a very valid concept that we must bear in mind. Certainly it is a possibility that we can go to either extreme. It's a most difficult thing to keep both intellect and emotion in some state of equilibrium.

Comment: I think that this is the very point of the humanities. If you are in the humanities you're not going to have this polarity because you are identifying yourself as an individual or you're looking at another person who has both of these elements in him. As he said, as soon as you intellectualize you come up with this dichotomy between mind and heart, body and soul, and destroy the person because the person is one. The real battle of the humanities is to look at the person as one. This is the difference between this morning and this afternoon. This morning we were on the idea of integration, of unity of the person, of the existential moment. This afternoon we come around and see a dual aspect. The humanities, I think, was truly this morning when we were going away from the technical. How to translate that into a learning situation with a classroom of students is another problem.

Comment: The fact remains that our main job is to teach students to make distinctions. For example, take two novels. If you don't teach that *The Collector* is not as great a work of art as *Crime and Punishment,* you have failed. The way to make the distinction is through the study of form, the techniques that Dostoevsky and Fowles use. Both books are psychological studies but why is one greater? Whether poetry, art or music, we are supposed to be teaching how to make distinctions. If we never bring a student beyond the point of "I like this poem and the other one is not good because I don't like it," we certainly have failed as teachers.

Comment: The most important thing about what I would present to the child is that he likes it and that he is impressed by it. However, later on when we talk about high school students and college students, I really do not know how you would ever get the beauty of any work of art unless you understand it. The full impact of a fugue cannot be understood unless you are able to follow a theme; you can never become an active listener unless you know something about, have an understanding for, the spirit or the mind of the century in which St. Peter ruled and a certain poem was written. That is the last enjoyment! This is actually what we *aim* at as we go through the school; it doesn't have to be done in kindergarten.

Comment: I can't help but rise in defense of Dr. De Mott, although I don't think he needs any defense. I don't think he was talking about not having a concern for form. I think he was saying that anybody has to get hooked first and see some relevance to himself, to his life and the world around him or it becomes some kind of academic, sterile matter. It's a distinction between teaching and learning. When a student begins to learn, when he really is hooked, then I think he will ask for the form, need the form, once more begin to hear what we are telling him. Actually is the humanistic approach also something beyond even intellectual and emotional sense of issues?—the issues "that rock" that Dr. Taylor was talking about? It is also something which makes clear the relativeness between the art and life, so that whoever it was that mentioned that the establishment may be disturbed with what we could do with the humanities is right? that if we carry the proposition all the way through to its logical conclusion people would begin to be human beings and it might be very disturbing to this world, but really great!

Comment: This morning I did not hear the fine distinction made in Professor De Mott's talk between things being good and bad. These were terms he deliberately avoided. We just had an appraisal here that we must be taught that certain novels are good. Then a student passes a course if he understands our criteria for a good novel and agrees with us. If he rejects it, we've defeated the purpose too. We're here trying to teach him to evaluate, not to decide what is good in art necessarily. He is going to draw up his own forms of what he thinks is good. He is going to have to appeal to them. You can give me a composition, you can explain it musically, I can understand it; if I still don't like it, it doesn't reach me. Now who is to say that Stravinsky is a better composer than Beethoven? I think we're on very thin grounds to say a student must recognize that this is good but this is better. He can set up his own criteria and show different methods of approach. Many of us would need a reorientation course on teen-age music, shall we say, or long haircuts. We've a hard time with some of these subjects in my ninth grade class. As one boy said the other day, "My father understands why I want my hair long. He sympathizes with me, but I still got to get it cut!" I don't think we can make these judgments. We have to show them how to make judgments for themselves. If they say they like it, okay, try to find out if they can tell us why they like it. We don't have to agree with them, but reading Dostoefsky leaves me very sad. I may reject his whole work; maybe I think something else is better, but I should have some idea why and this goes back to human beings understanding each other.

Comment: Unless we can define where Humanities will fit into the curriculum, we're still not going to teach the boy what two plus two is until he gets into high school and wants to take chemistry or geometry! In other words, we're not teaching this when he needs it; we're not going to teach him anything at the third grade. We're not going to teach him anything until he knows it! And if he gets in high school and decides he wants to take geometry, then we're going to teach him two plus two equals four, of course.

134

Current Non-Text Materials

in the

HUMANITIES

A BIBLIOGRAPHY

Marcia D. Starkey, *Bibliographer*

Part I   Classified Index by Subject

Part II Annotated List by Publisher

INTRODUCTION TO THE BIBLIOGRAPHY

The following bibliography has been compiled in response to numerous questions voiced by those attending the sessions of the Conference. It is an attempt to bring together some of the available materials which are either specifically directed toward the new social studies curricula or are, by nature, adaptable to use in such approaches.

Titles have been arranged in two sections. The second section is a classified index arranged by subject. Many titles are cross references and cross references to subjects have been provided. The first section is a list of titles arranged by publisher. Publishers' series have been grouped in an alphabetical arrangement.

Annotations have been provided either for series or individual title. Use or reading levels have been indicated when known, i.e.,: Jr. High, Advanced Placement, Secondary, Upper Elementary, Teacher, etc.

Only those titles were included for which examination copies were supplied by the publisher. This listing does not include all of the output of every publisher listed nor does it include titles from publishers who were unable to supply examination copies. The only exception is a title at present in press or projected and therefore unavailable.

We wish to acknowledge the support and cooperation of the publishers in supplying examination copies, in some cases their complete list in the social sciences.

CLASSIFIED INDEX

ARCHITECTURE – AMERICAN

Burchard, John and Bush-Brown, *The Architecture of America* (abridged) Little, Brown and Company, 1966, $3.95.

Robinson, Ethel Fay and Robinson, *Houses in America,* Viking Press, 1936, $4.13.

ARCHITECTURE – ARCHITECTS

Blake, Peter, *The Master Builders,* Knopf Publishers, Alfred A., 1966, $8.00.

Bush-Brown, Albert, *Louis Sullivan,* Braziller, George, 1960, $4.95.

Choay, Françoise, *Le Corbusier,* Braziller, George, 1960, $4.95.

Collins, George R., *Antonio Gaudí,* Braziller, George, 1960, $4.95.

Drexler, Arthur, *Ludwig Mies Van Der Rohe,* Braziller, George, 1960, $4.95.

Fitch, James Marston, *Walter Gropius,* Braziller, George, 1960, $4.95.

Forsee, Alyesa, *Frank Lloyd Wright: Rebel in Concrete,* Smith, Macrae, 1959, $4.95.

Gutheim, Frederick, *Alvar Aalto,* Braziller, George, 1960, $4.95.

Huxtable, Ada Louise, *Pier Luigi Nervi,* Braziller, George, 1960, $4.95.

McCoy, Esther, *Richard Neutra,* Braziller, George, 1960, $4.95.

Papadaki, Stamo, *Oscar Niemeyer,* Braziller, George, 1960, $4.95.

Scully, Jr., Vincent, *Frank Lloyd Wright,* Braziller, George, 1960, $4.95.

Von Eckardt, Wolf, *Eric Mendelsohn,* Braziller, George, 1960, $4.95.

ARCHITECTURE – MODERN

Crosby, Theo, *Architecture: City Sense,* Reinhold Publishing Corporation, 1965, $2.25.

Hitchcock, Henry-Russell, *Latin American Architecture Since 1945,* Simon and Schuster, 1955, $6.50.

Richards, J. M., *An Introduction to Modern Architecture,* Penguin Books, 1962, $1.25.

Scully, Jr., Vincent, *Modern Architecture,* Braziller, George, 1961, $4.95.

ARCHITECTURE – NATIONAL

Alex, William, *Japanese Architecture,* Braziller, George, 1963, $4.95.

Hoag, John D., *Western Islamic Architecture,* Braziller, George, 1963, $4.95.

Pevsner, Nikolaus, *An Outline of European Architecture,* Penguin Books, 1963, $2.25.

Wu, Nelson I., *Chinese and Indian Architecture*, Braziller, George, 1963, $4.95.

ARCHITECTURE – PERIOD

Banner, Robert, *Gothic Architecture*, Braziller, George, 1961, $4.95.

Brown, Frank E., *Roman Architecture*, Braziller, George, 1965, $4.95.

Lowry, Bates, *Renaissance Architecture*, Braziller, George, 1961, $4.95.

MacDonald, William, *Early Christian and Byzantine Architecture*, Braziller, George, 1962, $4.95.

Millon, Henry A., *Baroque and Rococo Architecture*, Braziller, George, 1961, $4.95.

Robertson, Donald, *Pre-Columbian Architecture*, Braziller, George, 1963, $4.95.

Saalman, Howard, *Medieval Architecture*, Braziller, George, 1962, $4.95.

Scranton, Robert L., *Greek Architecture*, Braziller, George, 1962, $4.95.

ARCHITECTURE – WORLD

Bergere, Thea and Richard, *From Stones to Skyscrapers: A Book About Architecture*, Dodd, Mead and Company, 1960, $3.50.

Donat, John, editor, *World Architecture*, volume 2, Viking Press, 1965, $15.00.

Hamlin, Talbot, *Architecture Thru the Ages*, Putnam's Sons, G. P., 1953, $9.50.

ART – GENERAL

Bloch, Raymond, *Etruscan Art*, New York Graphic Society, 1965, $10.00.

Cali, François, *The Spanish Arts of Latin America*, Viking Press, 1961, $12.50.

Chase, Alice Elizabeth, *Famous Artists of the Past*, Platt & Munk Publishers, Chanticleer Press, Inc., 1964, $6.39.

Coughlan, Robert and Time-Life Editors, *The World of Michelangelo, 1475–1564*, Time Incorporated, 1966, $4.95.

Dover, Cedric, *American Negro Art*, New York Graphic Society, 1960, $12.00.

Getlein, Frank and Dorothy, *Christianity in Modern Art*, Bruce Publishing Company, 1961, $5.00.

Gombrich, E. H., *The Story of Art*, Phaidon Press, Oxford University Press, 1966.

Harris, Neil, *The Artist in American Society: The Formative Years, 1790–1860*, Braziller, George, 1966, $7.50.

Hauser, Arnold, *The Social History of Art*, 4 volumes, Vintage Books, $1.45 each.

Hillier, J., *The Japanese Print: A New Approach,* Tuttle, 1960, $5.25.

Holme, Brian, *Drawings to Live With,* Viking Press, 1946, $4.13.

Morey, C. R., *Christian Art,* W. W. Norton and Company, Inc., 1935, $1.25.

Munro, Eleanor C., *The Encyclopedia of Art,* Golden Press, 1961, $9.95.

Munsterberg, Hugo, *The Arts of Japan: An Illustrated History,* Tuttle, 1962, $2.95.

Newton, Eric, *The Arts of Man,* New York Graphic Society, 1960, $5.95.

New York Graphic Society, *Music,* 1964, $7.95.

New York Graphic Society, *Man and Animal,* 1965, $7.95.

New York Graphic Society, *War and Peace,* 1964, $7.95.

Nicholas and others, *Art for Young America,* Bennett, Charles A., 1962.

Weiss, Paul, *World of Art,* Southern Illinois University Press, 1964, $4.50.

ART – INSTRUCTION, REFERENCE, AESTHETICS

Clapp, Jane, *Art in "Life",* Scarecrow Press, Inc., 1959, $12.50.

Clapp, Jane, *Art in "Life"*—supplement 1965, Scarecrow Press, Inc., 1965, $8.50.

Edman, Irwin, *Arts and the Man: A Short Introduction to Aesthetics,* W. W. Norton and Company, Inc., 1939, $1.85.

Jefferson, McGeary, Fredette, McGeary, *My World of Art,* Books 1–6, Allyn and Bacon, Inc., 1963, $2.12 each.

Kagan, Pauline Wright, *From Adventure to Experience Through Art,* Chandler Publishing Company, 1959, $2.25.

Maxcy, Kysar and Roberson, *Young Artists,* Books 1 thru 8, Merrill, Charles, 1959, $1.12.

Santayana, George, *The Sense of Beauty,* Dover Publications, Inc., 1955, $1.00.

Taylor, Joshua C., *Learning to Look: A Handbook for the Visual Arts,* University of Chicago Press, 1957, $1.95.

ART – MODERN

Baur, John I. H., editor, *New Art in America,* New York Graphic Society, 1957, $22.50.

Canaday, John, *Mainstreams of Modern Art,* Simon and Schuster, 1959, $15.00.

Carpenter, Edmund and others, *Eskimo,* University of Toronto Press, 1959, $3.95.

Cheney, Sheldon, *The Story of Modern Art,* Viking Press, 1958.

Goodrich, Lloyd and Baur, *American Art of Our Century,* Praeger, Frederick, 1961, $15.00.

Kuh, Katherine, *Break-up: The Core of Modern Art,* New York Graphic Society, 1965, $7.95.

Read, Herbert, *Art Now,* Pitman Publishing Company, 1960.

Sternberg, Harry, *Realistic/Abstract Art,* Pitman Publishing Company, 1959, $1.00.

ART – PAINTING

Ainaud, Juan, *Romanesque Painting,* Viking Press, 1963, $2.25.

Bazin, Germain, *French Impressionist Paintings in the Louvre,* Abrams, Inc., Harry N., 1966, $4.95.

Carli, Gudiol, and Souchal, *Gothic Painting,* Viking Press, 1965, $2.25.

Chatzidakis, Manolis and Grabar, *Byzantine and Early Medieval Painting,* Viking Press, 1965, $2.25.

Cogniat, Raymond, *17th Century Painting,* Viking Press, 1964, $2.25.

D'Espezel, Pierre and Fosca, *A Concise Illustrated History of European Painting,* Washington Square Press, 1961, $.90.

Devambez, Pierre, *Greek Painting,* Viking Press, 1962, $2.25.

DuBourguet, S. J., Pierre, *Early Christian Painting,* Viking Press, 1965, $2.25.

Flezner, James Thomas, *The Pocket History of American Painting,* Washington Square Press, 1950, $.60.

Geldzahler, Henry, *American Painting in the 20th Century,* Metropolitan Museum of Art, New York Graphic Society, 1965, $7.50.

Goodrich, Lloyd, *Albert Ryder,* Braziller, George, 1959, $4.95.

Goossen, E. C., *Stuart Davis,* Braziller, George, 1959, $4.95.

Gore, Frederick, *Painting: Some Basic Principles,* Reinhold Publishing Company, 1965, $2.25.

Hess, Thomas B., *Willem De Kooning,* Braziller, George, 1959, $4.95.

Holme, Bryan, Pictures to Live With, Viking Press, 1959, $4.50.

Hunter, Sam, *Modern American Painting and Sculpture,* Dell Publishing Company, 1959, $.95.

Hunter, Sam, *Modern French Painting: 50 Artists From Manet to Picasso,* Dell Publishing Company, 1956, $.95.

Jaffe, H. L. C., *Twentieth Century Painting,* Viking Press, 1963, $2.25.

Janson and Janson, *The Picture History of Painting,* Washington Square Press, 1961, $1.45.

Janson and Janson, *The Story of Painting for Young People,* Abrams, Inc., Harry N., No Date.

Kramer, Nora, editor, *The Grandma Moses Storybook,* Random House Press, 1961, $5.95.

McCoubrey, John W., *American Tradition in Painting*, Braziller, George, 1963, $4.95.

Mitchell, Sabrina, *Medieval Manuscript Painting*, Viking Press, 1964, $2.25.

O'Hara, Frank, *Jackson Pollock*, Braziller, Goerge, 1959, $4.95.

Peillex, Georges, *Nineteenth Century Painting*, Viking Press, 1964, $2.25.

Photiades, Wassily, *18th Century Painting*, Viking Press, 1963, $2.25.

Porter, Fairfield, *Thomas Eakins*, Braziller, George, 1959, $4.95.

Rosenberg, Jakob, *Rembrandt: Life and Work*, Phaidon Publishers, Inc. New York Graphic Society, 1964, $8.50.

Russoli Franco, *Renaissance Painting*, Viking Press, 1962, $2.25.

Seuphor, Michael, *Abstract Painting*, Dell Publishing Company, 1964, $.95.

Stenico, Arturo, *Roman and Etruscan Painting*, Viking Press, 1963, $2.25.

Toda, Kenji, *Japanese Painting: A Brief History*, Tuttle Publishing Company, 1965, $2.50.

ART – PRIMITIVE AND FOLK

Bailey, C. S., *Pioneer Art in America*, Viking Press, 1944, $4.13.

Covarrubias, Miguel, *The Eagle, the Jaguar and the Serpent; Indian Arts of the Americas*, Knopf, Albert A., 1954, $15.00.

Dockstader, Frederick J., *Indian Art in America*, New York Graphic Society, 1962, $25.00.

Emmerich, Andre, *Art Before Columbus*, Simon and Schuster, 1963, $10.00.

Krevitsky, Nik, *Batik: Art and Craft*, Reinhold Publishing Corp., 1964, $5.50.

Museum of Primitive Art, *Masterpieces in the Museum of Primitive Art*, New York Graphic Society, 1965, $4.95.

Museum of Primitive Art, *Traditional Art of the African Nations in the Museum of Primitive Art*, University Publishers, 1961, $6.00.

Myron, Robert, *Prehistoric Art*, Pitman Publishers Co., 1964, $1.00.

Sabine, Ellen S., *American Folk Art*, Van Nostrand Co., Inc., 1958, $8.95.

Stewart, Janice S., *The Folk Arts of Norway*, University of Wisconsin Press, 1953, $10.00.

ART – SCULPTURE

Ford, Betty Davenport, *Ceramic Sculpture*, Reinhold Publishing Company, 1964, $5.50.

Goldwater, Robert, *Senufo Sculpture From West Africa*, Museum of Primitive Art, New York Graphic Society, 1964, $8.95.

Myers, Bernard, *Sculpture: Form and Method,* Reinhold Publishing Company, 1965, $2.25.

Sergy, Ladislas, *African Sculpture,* Dover Publishing Company, 1958, $2.00.

CULTURE – GENERAL

Bagby, Philip, *Culture and History,* University of California Press, 1963, $1.50.

Cassirer, Ernst, *An Essay on Man: An Introduction to a Philosophy of Human Culture,* Yale University Press, 1944, $1.75.

Cottrell, Leonard, *The Horizon Book of Lost Worlds,* Dell Publishing Company, 1962, $.75.

Dobler, Lavinia, *Customs and Holidays Around the World,* Fleet Publishing Corporation, 1962, $4.50.

Habberton, Roth and Spears, *World History and Culture: The Story of Man's Achievements,* Laidlaw Brothers, 1966.

"Horizon" Eds. *The Light of the Past,* American Heritage Publishing Company, Simon and Schuster, 1965, $13.95.

Laver, James, *Costume Through the Ages,* Simon and Schuster, 1963, $4.95.

"Life" Editors, *The World's Great Religions,* Golden Press, 1958.

Lynch, Patrick, *Man Makes His World,* Saint Martin's Press, 1959.

Steward, Julian H., *Theory of Culture Change,* University of Illinois, (1955) 1963.

White, Leslie A., *The Science of Culture: A Study of Man and Civilization,* Grove Press, 1949, $2.95.

CULTURE – NON-WESTERN

Buell, Hal, *Festivals of Japan,* Dodd, Mead and Co., 1965, $2.99.

Ch'u Chai and Winberg Chai, editors, *The Humanist Way in Ancient China: Essential Works of Confucianism,* Bantam Publishing Company, 1965, $.95.

Cottrell, Leonard, *Realms of Gold,* New York Graphic Society, 1963, $5.95.

Cottrell, Leonard, *The Secrets of Tutankhamen's Tomb,* New York Graphic Society, 1964, $4.50.

Crawford, Ann Caddell, *Customs and Culture of Vietnam,* Tuttle Publishing Company, 1966, $3.95.

Dean, Vera Micheles, *The Nature of the Non-Western World,* New American Library/Mentor, 1966, $.75.

DeBary, William, editor, *Sources of Chinese Tradition,* 2 volumes, Columbia University Press, 1960, $3.50, $2.50 ea.

DeBary, William, editor, *Sources of Japanese Tradition,* 2 volumes, Columbia University Press, 1958, $3.25, $2.75 ea.

DeBary, William, editor, *Sources of Indian Tradition,* 2 volumes, Columbia University Press, 1958, $3.25, $2.75 ea.

Diez, Ernst, *The Ancient Worlds of Asia: From Mesopotamia to the Yellow River*, G. P. Putnam's Sons, 1961, $4.50.

Jahn, Janheinz, *Muntu: The New African Culture*, Grove Press, 1961, $2.45.

Mendelsohn, Jack, *God, Allah and Ju Ju*, Nelson and Sons, Thomas, 1962, $3.75.

Mertz, Barbara, Temples, *Tombs and Hieroglyphs*, Dell Publishing Company, 1964, $1.95.

Ottenberg, Simon and Phoebe, editors, *Cultures and Societies of Africa*, Random House, 1960.

Sansom, G. B., *Japan: A Short Cultural History*, Appleton-Century Crofts, Inc., 1962, $5.75.

Zabilka, Gladys, *Customs and Culture of Okinawa*, Tuttle Publishing Company, 1959, ($1.50), $3.95.

Zabilka, Gladys, *Customs and Culture of the Philippines*, Tuttle Publishing Company, 1963, ($1.50), $3.95.

CULTURE – WESTERN

American Heritage, editors, *The American Heritage Book of Indians*, American Heritage Publishing Company, Simon and Schuster, 1961, $15.00.

Bowra, C. M. and Time-Life editors, *Classical Greece*, Time, Inc., 1965, $3.95.

Brantl, Ruth, editor, *Medieval Culture*, Braziller, George, 1966, $6.95.

Dorra, Henri, *The American Muse*, Viking Press, 1961, $10.00.

Hunt and Carlson, *Masks and Mask Makers*, Association Press, 1961, $3.00.

Macfarlan, Allan A., *Book of American Indian Games*, Association Press, 1958, $3.95.

Mates, J. and Cantelupe, editors, *Renaissance Culture*, Braziller, George, 1966, $6.95.

Paz, Octavio, *The Labyrinth of Solitude: Life and Thought in Mexico*, Grove Press, Inc., 1961, $1.95.

Peckham, Morse, editor, *Romanticism*, Braziller, George, 1965, $6.95.

Phelps, Robert, editor, *20th Century* Culture, Braziller, George, 1965, $6.95.

Schneider, Isidor, editor, *The Enlightenment*, Braziller, George, 1965, $6.95.

Silverberg, Robert, *The Old Ones: Indians of the American South West*, New York Graphic Society, 1965, $4.95.

Stefansson, Evelyn, *Here is Alaska*, Scribner Publishing Company, 1959.

Von Hildebrand, Alice, editor, *Greek Culture*, Braziller, George, 1966, $6.95.

Weinstein, Leo, editor, *The Age of Reason*, Braziller, George, 1965, $6.95.

Wills, Garry, editor, *Roman Culture*, Braziller, George, 1966, $6.95.

DRAMA

Abbott, A. S., *Shaw and Christianity*, Seabury Press, 1965, $4.95.

Brown, Ivor, *How Shakespeare Spent the Day*, Hill and Wang, 1963, ($1.65), $5.00.

Chekhov, O'Casey, Miller, Ibsen, Shaw and Williams, *Six Great Modern Plays*, Dell Publishing Company, 1956, $.75.

Clark, J. Kent and Piper, Henry Dan, editors, *Dimensions in Drama: Six Plays of Crime and Punishment*, Scribner's Sons, 1964.

Clurman, Harold, editor, *Famous American Plays of the 1930's*, Dell Publishers, 1959, $.75.

Corrigan, Robert W., editor, *Laurel British Drama: The Twentieth Century*, Dell Publishers, 1965, $.95.

DeMille, A. B., *Three English Comedies*, Allyn and Bacon, 1924–1965.

Flores, Angel, editor, *Spanish Drama*, Bantam Books, 1962, $.75.

Fowlie, Wallace, editor and translator, *Classical French Drama*, Bantam Books, 1962, $.60.

Freedley, George, editor, *Three Plays by Maxwell Anderson*, Washington Square Press, 1962. $.60.

Frenz, Horst, editor, *American Playwrights on Drama*, Hill and Wang, 1965, ($1.65), $3.95.

Gassner, John, editor, *Four Great Elizabethan Plays*, Bantam Books, 1960, $.75.

Gassner, John, editor, *Medieval and Tudor Drama*, Bantam Books, 1963, $1.25.

Goldsmith, Sheridan, Beach and Barry, *Comparative Comedies: She Stoops to Conquer, The Rivals, The Goose Hangs High, Holiday*, Noble and Noble, 1953.

Hewes, Henry, editor, *Famous American Plays of the 1940's*, Dell Publishing Company, 1960, $.75.

Houghton, Norris, editor, *Great Russian Plays*, Dell Publishing Company, $.75.

Houghton, Norris, editor, *The Romantic Influence*, Dell Publishing Company, 1963, $.95.

Houghton, Norris, editor, *Seeds of Modern Drama*, Dell Publishing Company, 1963, $.75.

Hurrell, John D., *Two Modern American Tragedies*, Scribner's Sons, 1961.

144

Jonson, Ben, *Three Comedies,* Penguin Books, 1966, $1.45.

Konick, Marcus, *Six Complete World Plays and A History of World Drama,* Globe Book Company, 1963, $3.96.

MacCann, Richard Dyer, *Film and Society,* Scribner's Sons, Charles, 1964.

MacGowan, Kenneth, editor, *Famous American Plays of the 1920's,* Dell Publishing Company, 1959, $.75.

Markels, Julian, *Shakespeare's "Julius Caesar",* Scribner's Sons, Charles, 1961.

Mersand, Joseph, editor, *Three Plays about Doctors,* Washington Square Press, 1961, $.60.

Mersand, Joseph, editor, *Three Plays about Marriage,* Washington Square Press, 1962, $.60.

Mersand, Joseph, editor, *Three Dramas of American Individualism,* Washington Square Press, 1961, $.60.

Mersand, Joseph, editor, *Three Dramas of American Realism,* Washington Square Press, 1961, $.60.

Moon, Samuel, editor, *One Act: II Short Plays of Modern Theatre,* Grove Press, 1961, $1.95.

Shakespeare, William, and Anderson, *Julius Caesar—Elizabeth the Queen,* Noble and Noble, 1958.

Shakespeare, William, and Balderson, *A Midsummer Night's Dream—Berkeley Square,* Noble and Noble, 1963.

Shakespeare, William, and O'Neill, *Macbeth—The Emperor Jones,* Noble and Noble, 1965.

Shakespeare, William, and Rostand, *Romeo and Juliet—Cyrano de Bergerac,* Noble and Noble, 1965.

Shakespeare, William, Sophocles and O'Neill, *Hamlet—Electra—Beyond the Horizon,* Noble and Noble, 1966.

Shakespeare, William, *Hamlet,* Washington Square Press, 1966, $.75.

Sheratsky, R. and Reilly, *The Lively Arts: 4 Representative Types,* Globe Book Company, 1964, $4.20.

Stafford, William T., *James's "Daisy Miller",* Scribner's Sons, Charles, 1963.

Strasberg, Lee, *Famous American Plays of the 1950's,* Dell Publishing Company, 1962, $.75.

Tourneur, Webster and Middleton, *The Three Jacobean Tragedies,* Penguin Books, 1965, $.95.

Wilde, Oscar. *Five Plays by Oscar Wilde,* Bantam Books, 1961, $.95.

Wilder, Thornton, *Three Plays by Thornton Wilder,* Bantam Books, 1966, $.75.

Yurka, Blanche, editor, *Three Scandinavian Plays,* Washington Square Press, 1962, $.60.

FOLKLORE – CLASSICAL

Gayley, Charles Mills, editor, *The Classic Myths in English Literature and Art,* Blaisdell Publishing Company, 1939.

Guerber, H. A., *Myths of Greece and Rome,* American Book Company, 1921.

Leach, Maria, *The Beginning: Creation Myths Around the World,* Funk and Wagnalls, 1956, $3.75.

Sabin, Frances E., *Classical Myths that Live Today,* Silver Burdett Company, 1958.

White, Anne Terry, *The Golden Treasury of Myths and Legend,* Golden Press, 1959.

FOLKLORE – NON-WESTERN

Brown, Marcia, *The Flying Carpet,* Scribner's Sons, Charles, 1956, $2.65.

Campbell, Joseph, *The Masks of God, Oriental Mythology,* Viking Press, 1962, $7.50.

Chang, Isabelle C., *Chinese Fairy Tales,* Barre Publishers, 1965, $4.95.

Davis, Russell and Ashabranner, *The Lion's Whiskers,* Little, Brown and Company, 1959, $3.95.

DeLeeuw, *Indonesian Legends and Folk Tales,* Nelson and Sons, Thomas, 1961.

Dolch and Dolch, *Stories from Hawaii,* Garrard Publishing Company, 1960, $2.49.

Dolch, *Stories from India,* Garrard Publishing Company, 1961, $2.49.

Dolch, *Stories from Japan,* Garrard Publishing Company, 1960, $2.49.

Dolch, *Stories from Old China,* Garrard Publishing Company, 1964, $2.49.

Dolch, *Stories from Old Egypt,* Garrard Publishing Company, 1964, $2.49.

Dorson, Richard M., *Folk Legends of Japan,* Tuttle Publishing Company, 1962, $4.75.

Feldmann, Susan, editor, *African Myths and Tales,* Dell Publishing Company, 1963, $.50.

Kim So-Un, *The Story Bag: A Collection of Korean Folktales,* Tuttle Publishing Company, 1955, $1.50.

O'Donnell, J. E., *Japanese Folk Tales,* Caxton Printers, Ltd., 1958, $3.50.

Sakade, Florence, editor, *Japanese Children's Favorite Stories,* Tuttle Publishing Company, 1958, $3.50.

Uchida, Yoshiko, *The Sea of Gold and Other Tales from Japan,* Scribner's Sons, Charles, 1965.

FOLKLORE – WESTERN

Asbjornsen and Moe, *Norwegian Folk Tales*, Viking Press, 1960, $4.53.

Brown, Marcia, *Once a Mouse . . . A Fable Cut in Wood*, Scribner's Sons, Charles, 1961, $3.12.

Clark, Eleanor, *The Song of Roland*, Random House, 1960, $1.50.

Cooney, Barbara, *The Little Juggler*, Hastings House, 1961, $3.25.

Cothran, Jean, editor, *The Magic Calabash: Folk Tales from America's Islands and Alaska*, McKay Company, Inc., 1956, $2.95.

DeOsma, Lupe, *The Witches' Ride and Other Tales from Costa Rica*, Morrow and Company, Willam, 1957, $3.00.

Dolch, *Stories From Alaska*, Garrard Publishing Company, 1961, $2.49.

Dolch, *Stories From Canada*, Garrard Publishing Company, 1964, $2.49.

Dolch, *Stories From France*, Garrard Publishing Company, 1963, $2.49.

Dolch, *Stories From Italy*, Garrard Publishing Company, 1962, $2.49.

Dolch, *Stories From Mexico*, Garrard Publishing Company, 1960, $2.49.

Dolch, *Stories From Old Russia*, Garrard Publishing Company, 1964, $2.49.

Dolch, *Stories From Spain*, Garrard Publishing Company, 1962, $2.49.

Dorson, Richard, *American Folklore*, University of Chicago Press, 1959, $1.95.

Eells, Elsie Spicer, *Tales From the Amazon*, Dodd, Mead and Company, 1965, $3.00.

Feldmann, Susan, editor, *The Story-Telling Stone: Myths and Tales of the American Indians*, Dell Publishing Company, 1965, $.60.

Gimbutas, Marija, *Ancient Symbolism in Lithuanian Folk Art*, American Folklore Society, University of Texas Press, 1958.

Grimm Brothers, *The Shoemaker and the Elves*, Scribner's Sons, Charles, 1960.

Holl, Adelaide, *Magic Tales*, Merrill, Charles, 1964, $2.64.

Hughes, Langston and Bontemps, editors, *The Book of Negro Folklore*, Dodd, Mead and Company, 1966.

Jennings, Gary, *Black Magic, White Magic*, Dial Press, 1964, $3.75.

McKendry, John H., editor, *Aesop: Five Centuries of Illustrated Fables*, Metropolitan Museum of Art, New York Graphic Society, 1964, $4.95.

147

MacManus, Seumas, *The Bold Heroes of Hungry Hill and Other Irish Folk Tales,* Farrar, Straus and Giroux, 1951, $2.95.

Olsen, Ib Spang, *The Marsh Crone's Brew,* Abington Press, 1960, $1.50.

Potter and Gilbert, *Giants and Fairies,* Merrill, Charles E., 1964, $2.64.

Potter and Harley, *First Fairy Tales,* Merrill, Charles E., 1964, $2.64.

Ressler, Theodore Whitson, *Treasury of American Indian Tales,* Association Press, 1957, $3.95.

LANGUAGE

Bryant, Margaret M., *Current American Usage,* Funk and Wagnalls, 1962, $5.00.

Fraenkel, Gerd, *What Is Language?,* Ginn and Company, 1965.

Funk, Wilfred, *Word Origins and Their Romantic Stories,* Grosset and Dunlap, 1950.

Hofsinde, Robert, *Indian Sign Language,* Morrow Publishing Company, 1956, $2.75.

Malmstrom, Jean and Ashley, Annabel, *Dialects, U.S.A.,* National Council of Teachers of English, 1963, $2.25.

Shanker, Sidney, *Semantics: The Magic of Words,* Ginn and Company, 1965.

LITERATURE – CRITICAL ESSAYS

Baker, Carlos, *Ernest Hemingway,* Scribner's Sons, Charles, 1962.

Cicero, *Selected Works* (revised), Penguin Books, 1965, $.95.

Cowley and Cowley, *Fitzgerald and The Jazz Age,* Scribner's Sons, Charles, 1966.

Ferres, John H., editor, *Sherwood Anderson: Winesburg, Ohio,* Viking Press, 1966, $1.95.

Holman, C. Hugh, *The World of Thomas Wolfe,* Scribner's Sons, Charles, 1962.

Kazin, Alfred and Aaron, editors, *Emerson: A Modern Anthology,* Dell Publishing Company, 1958, $.50.

McDermott, John Francis, editor, *The World of Washington Irving,* Dell Publishing Company, 1965, $.50.

Weintraub, Stanley *C. P. Snow: A Spectrum,* Scribner's Sons, Charles, 1963.

LITERATURE – NOVEL

Austen, Jane, *Emma,* Penguin Books, 1966, $1.25.

Austen, Jane, *Mansfield Park,* Penguin Books, 1966, $1.45.

Austen, Jane, *Persuasion,* Penguin Books, 1965, $.95.

Bronte, Charlotte, *Jane Eyre,* Penguin Books, 1966, $.95.

Bronte, Emily, *Wuthering Heights,* Penguin Books, 1965, $.95.

Bunyan, John, *The Pilgrim's Progress*, Penguin Books, 1965, $.95.

Butler, Samuel, *The Way of All Flesh*, Penguin Books, 1966, $.95.

Collins, Wilkie, *The Moonstone*, Penguin Books, 1966, $1.25.

Day, Clarence, *Life With Mother*, Washington Square Press, 1965, $.60.

Defoe, Daniel, *A Journal of the Plague Year*, Penguin Books, 1966, $.95.

Defoe, Daniel, *Robinson Crusoe*, Penguin Books, 1965, $.95.

Defoe, Daniel, *Robinson Crusoe*, Washington Square Press, 1963, $.60.

Defoe, Trumbull, Coleridge, *The Rime of the Ancient Mariner*, Noble and Noble, 1965.

Dickens, Charles, *David Copperfield*, Penguin Books, 1966, $1.95.

Dickens, Charles, *Great Expectations*, Penguin Books, 1965, $1.25.

Dickens, Charles, *Oliver Twist*, Penguin Books, 1966, $1.45.

Dickens and Steinberg, *A Tale of Two Cities—The Moon Is Down*. Noble and Noble, 1965.

Drew, Elizabeth, *The Novel: A Modern Guide to 15 English Masterpieces*, Dell Publishing Company, 1963. $.60.

DuMaurier, Daphne, *Rebecca*, Washington Square Press, 1965, $.75.

Eliot, George, *Middlemarch*, Penguin Books, 1965, $1.45.

Eliot, George, *Silas Marner*, Washington Square Press, 1964, $.40.

Eliot and Steinbeck, *Silas Marner—The Pearl*, Noble and Noble, 1965.

Fielding, Henry, *Tom Jones*, Penguin Books, 1966, $1.65.

Hardy, Thomas, *The Mayor of Casterbridge*, Washington Square Press, 1964, $.75.

Hardy, Thomas, *The Return of the Native*, Washington Square Press, 1964, $.75.

Hawthorne, Nathaniel, *The Scarlet Letter*, Washington Square Press, 1963, $.60.

Konopnicka, Marcia, *The Golden Seed*, Scribner's Sons, Charles, 1962, $3.31.

Landon, Margaret, *Anna and the King of Siam* (abridged edition) Washington Square Press, 1963, $.75.

London, Jack, *The Call of the Wild*, Washington Square Press, 1963, $.60.

Melville, Herman, *Melville: The Best of Moby Dick and Typee: Billy Budd Complete*, Platt and Munk, 1964, $3.97.

Mitchell, Margaret, *Gone With the Wind*, Pocket Books, 1964, $1.25.

Pflug, Raymond J., *The Adventures of Huckleberry Finn: Evolution of a Classic*, Ginn and Company, 1965.

Popp, Lilian M., *4 Complete Heritage Novels*, Globe Book Company, 1963, $4.20.

Popp, Lilian M., *4 Complete Modern Novels*, Globe Book Company, 1962, $4.20.

Popp, Lilian M., *4 Complete Novels of Character and Courage*, Globe Book Company, 1964, $4.20.

Steinbeck, John, *The Pearl and The Red Pony*, Viking Press, 1965, $1.25.

Stevenson, R. L., *Treasure Island*, Washington Square Press, 1963, $.60.

Turgenev, *Fathers and Sons*, Bantam Books, 1959, $.60.

Twain, Mark, *The Adventures of Huckleberry Finn*, Penguin Books, 1966, $1.25.

Twain, Mark, *The Adventures of Tom Sawyer*, Houghton Mifflin Company, 1962.

Twain, Mark, *The Adventures of Tom Sawyer*, Washington Square Press, 1963, $.60.

Twain, Mark, *The Adventures of Tom Sawyer, The Adventures of Huckleberry Finn*, Platt and Munk, 1960, $3.97.

Verne, Jules, *20,000 Leagues Under the Sea* and *Around the Moon*, Platt and Munk, 1965, $3.97.

LITERATURE – GENERAL WORKS

Arbuthnot, May Hill, *The Arbuthnot Anthology of Children's Literature*, Scott, Foresman and Company, 1961.

Ellman, Richard and Feidelson, Jr., editors, *The Modern Tradition*, Oxford University Press, 1965.

Flores, Angel, editor, *Medieval Age*, Dell Publishing Company, 1963, $.95.

Read, Warren, W., *Comparative Essays: Present and Past*, Noble and Noble, 1965.

Stern, Milton R. and Gross, editors, *American Literature Survey*, Viking Press, 1962, $1.75.

LITERATURE – SHORT STORY

Auden, W. H. editor, *The Portable Greek Reader*, Viking Press, 1948, $1.85.

Bellow, Saul, editor, *Great Jewish Short Stories*, Dell Publishing Company, 1963, $.50.

Brinton, Crane, editor, *The Portable Age of Reason Reader*, Viking Press, 1956, $1.85.

Conrad, Joseph, *Three Short Novels*, Bantam Books, 1960, $.50.

Crane, Milton, editor, *50 Great American Short Stories*, Bantam Books, 1965, $.95.

Davenport, Basil, editor, *The Portable Roman Reader*, Viking Press, 1951, $1.85.

DeOnis, Harriet, editor, *Spanish Stories and Tales*, Washington Square Press, 1962, $.45.

Doyle, Sir Arthur Conan, *Conan Doyle Stories*, Pratt and Munk, 1960, $3.97.

Geismar, Maxwell, editor, *Jack London: Short Stories*, Hill and Wang, 1960, $1.75.

Goodman, Roger B., *World-Wide Short Stories*, Globe Book Company, 1966, $3.00.

Hanrahan, Gene Z., editor, *50 Great Oriental Stories*, Bantam Books, 1965, $.95.

Hansen, Harry, editor, *The Pocket Book of O. Henry Stories*, Washington Square Press, 1948, $.45.

Harte, Bret, *Stories of the Early West*, Platt and Munk, 1964, $3.97.

Hugo, Howard E., editor, *The Portable Romantic Reader*, Viking Press, 1957, $1.85.

Joyce, James, *The Cat and the Devil*, Dodd, Mead and Company, 1964, $3.50.

Kipling, Rudyard, *Kipling Stories: 28 Tales*, Platt and Munk, 1960, $3.97.

London, Jack, *Jack London Stories*, Platt and Munk, 1960, $3.97.

McAndrew, Andrew R., editor, *Four Soviet Masterpieces*, Bantam Books, 1965, $.95.

Mercier, Vivian, editor, *Great Irish Short Stories*, Dell Publishing Company, 1964, $.60.

Morris, Ivan, editor, *Modern Japanese Stories: An Anthology*, Tuttle Company, Charles E., 1962, $6.50.

O. Henry, *O. Henry Stories*, Platt and Munk, 1962, $3.97.

Pasinetti, P. M., editor, *Great Italian Short Stories*, Dell Publishing Company, 1959, $.60.

Poe, Edgar Allan, *Edgar Allan Poe Stories*, Platt and Munk, 1961, $3.97.

Reeve, S. D., editor, *Great Soviet Short Stories*, Dell Publishing Company, 1962, $.75.

Ross, J. B. and McLaughlin, editors, *The Portable Medieval Reader*, Viking Press, 1949, $1.85.

Ross, J. B. and McLaughlin, editors, *The Portable Renaissance Reader*, Viking Press, 1953, $1.85.

Scherer, Margaret R., *The Legends of Troy in Art and Literature* (2nd edition), Phaidon Press–Metropolitan Museum of Art, 1964, $7.95.

Spector, Robert Donald, editor, *Seven Masterpieces of Gothic Horror*, Bantam Books, 1963, $.95.

Spender, Stephen, editor, *Great German Short Stories*, Dell Publishing Company, 1960, $.50.

151

Stevenson, Robert Louis, *Great Tales of Mystery and Adventure*, Platt and Munk, 1965, $3.97.

Turgenev, Tolstoy, Dostoyevsky and Chekhov, *Four Great Russian Short Novels*, Dell Publishing Company, 1959, $.50.

Twain, Mark, *The Complete Short Stories of Mark Twain*, Bantam Books, 1957, $.95.

Van Buitenen, J, A. B., editor, *Tales of Ancient India*, Bantam Books, 1959, $.50.

Warren, Robert Penn and Erskine, editors, *Short Story Masterpieces*, Dell Publishing Company, 1954, $.75.

Wells, H. G., *The War of the Worlds, The Time Machine, Selected Short Stories*, Platt and Munk, 1963, $3.97.

LITERATURE – TECHNIQUE AND CRITICISM

Davenport, William H. and Siegel, editors, *Biography: Past and Present—Selections and Critical Essays*, Scribner's Sons, Charles, 1965.

Kane, Thomas S. and Peters, editors, *Writing Prose: Techniques and Purposes* (2nd edition), Oxford University Press, 1964.

Keene, Donald, *Japanese Literature: An Introduction for Western Readers*, Grove Press, 1955, $1.45.

Leary, Lewis, editor, *The Teacher and American Literature*, National Council of Teachers of English, 1965, $2.25.

Litz, A. Walton, editor, *Modern American Fiction: Essays in Criticism*, Oxford University Press, 1963, $2.25.

Pannwitt, Barbara, editor, *The Art of Short Fiction*, Ginn and Company, 1964.

Proust, Marcel, *Marcel Proust on Art and Literature: 1896–1919*, Dell Publishing Company, 1964, $2.25.

West, William W., editor, *On Writing, By Writers*, Ginn and Company, 1966.

LITERATURE – TEXTBOOKS

Chase-Jewett and Evans, editors, *Values in Literature*, Houghton Mifflin Company, 1965.

Holder and others, editors, *Journeys in American Literature*, Globe Book Company, 1958, $4.36.

Horn, Gunnar, *A Cavalcade of American Writing*, Allyn and Bacon, 1966.

Horn, Gunnar, *A Cavalcade of British* Writing, Allyn and Bacon, 1961.

Horn, Gunnar, *A Cavalcade of World Writing*, Allyn and Bacon, 1966.

Jacobs, Johnson and Turner, editors, *Seesaw*, Merrill, Charles E., 1966, $2.20.

Jacobs, Johnson and Turner, editors, *Merry-Go-Round*, Grade 1, Merrill, Charles E., 1966, $2.72.

Jacobs, Johnson and Turner, editors, *Happiness Hill*, Grade 2, Merrill, Charles E., 1966, $2.96.

Jacobs, Johnson and Turner, editors, *Treat Shop*, Grade 3, Merrill, Charles E., $3.12.

Jacobs, Johnson and Turner, editors, *Magic Carpet*, Grade 4, Merrill, Charles E., $3.28.

Jacobs, Johnson and Turner, editors, *Enchanted Isles*, Grade 5, Merrill, Charles E., $3.40.

Jacobs, Johnson and Turner, editors, *Adventure Lands*, Grade 6, Merrill, Charles E., $3.52.

Pooley, Robert C., editor, *England in Literature*, Scott, Foresman, 1963, $4.29, $1.29, $.72.

Pooley, Robert C., editor, *Exploring Life Thru Literature*, Scott, Foresman, 1964, $3.93, $1.20, $.66.

Pooley, Robert C., editor, *Outlooks Thru Literature*, Scott, Foresman, 1964, $3.87, $.93, $.63.

Pooley, Robert C., editor, *The U. S. in Literature*, Scott, Foresman, 1963, $4.14, $1.20, $.72.

Shapiro, Alan, *American Literature—Four Representative Types*, Globe Book Company, 1964, $4.20.

Sullivan, Catherine J., *A Cavalcade of Life in Writing*, Allyn and Bacon, 1963.

MUSIC

Ames, Russell, *The Story of American Folksong*, Grossett and Dunlap, 1960.

Baines, Anthony, editor, *Musical Instruments Thru the Ages*, Walker and Company, 1961, $10.00.

Best, Florence C., *Music in the Making*: a workbook for General Music Classes, Summy-Birchard Company, 1960, $2.80.

Bissell, K., *Festival Songs for S.A.B.*, Waterloo Music Company, Ltd., 1961.

Buker, Alden, *A Humanistic Approach to Music Appreciation*, National Press, 1964.

Buker, Alden, *A Social Approach to Music Appreciation*, National Press, 1963.

Cooper and others, *Music in Our Life*, Silver Burdett Company, 1967, $3.76, $4.80, text edition.

Cooper and others, *Music in Our Times*, Silver Burdett Company, 1967, $3.84 text edition, $4.80 teacher's edition.

Fowke and Johnston, *Folk Songs of Canada* (choral edition), Waterloo Music Company, Ltd., 1954.

Fowke and Johnston, *Folksongs of Quebec* (melody edition), Waterloo Music Company, Ltd., 1958.

Friedman, Albert B., editor, *The Viking Book of Folk Ballads of the English Speaking World,* Viking Press, 1956, $2.25.

Grout, Donald Jay, *A History of Western Music* (shorter edition), Norton and Company, Inc., 1964.

Jackson, George Pullen, editor, *Spiritual Folk Songs of Early America,* Dover Publishing Company, 1964, $2.00.

Johnston, Richard, arranger, *Chansons Canadiennes—Francaises* (French-Canadian Songs), Waterloo Music Company, Ltd., 1964.

Kelly, Jr., John M, *Folk Songs Hawaii Sings,* Tuttle Publishing Company, 1962, $4.95.

Kettelkamp, Larry, *Drums, Rattles and Bells,* Morrow and Company, William, 1960.

McGenee and Nelson, *People and Music* (revised), Allyn and Bacon, 1966.

McKinney, Howard D., *Music and Man,* American Book Company, 1962.

Pawlowska, Harriet M., editor, *Merrily We Sing: 105 Polish Folksongs,* Wayne State University Press, 1961.

Peyser, Ethel and Bauer, *How Opera Grew,* Putnam's Sons, G. P., 1956, $6.00.

Serposs, Emile H. and Singleton, *Music in Our Heritage,* Silver Burdett Company, 1962, $4.00.

Shippen, Katherine B. and Seidlova, *The Heritage of Music,* Viking Press, 1963, $5.63.

Slavita, Chana, *Let's Go to a Ballet,* Putnam's Sons, G. P., 1959.

Wakefield, Eleanor Ely, *Folk Dancing in America,* Pratt and Company, J. Lowell, 1966, $3.95.

POETRY

Allen, Donald M., editor, *The New American Poetry,* Grove Press, Inc., 1960, $2.95.

Arnstein, Flora J., *Poetry in the Elementary Classroom,* National Council of Teachers of English/Appleton-Century-Crofts, 1962, $2.95.

Austin and Mills, *The Sound of Poetry,* Allyn and Bacon, 1964.

Bogan, Louise and Smith, editors, *The Golden Journey; Poems for Young People,* Reilley and Lee Company, 1965, $5.95.

Bowra, C. M., *Heroic Poetry,* Saint Martin's Press, 1964.

Brinnin, John Malcolm, editor, *Emily Dickinson,* Dell Publishing Company, 1960, $.35.

Cooke, Olivia M., editor, *Comparative Narrative Poetry: Present and Past,* Noble and Noble, 1965.

Crane, Milton, editor, *50 Great Poets,* Bantam Books, Inc., 1961, $1.25.

Drew, Elizabeth, *Poetry: A Modern Guide to its Understanding and Enjoyment*, Dell Publishing Company, 1959, $.50.

Grigson, Geoffrey, *Poets in their Pride*, Basic Books, Inc., 1964, $4.95.

Hall, Donald, editor, *Contemporary American Poets*, Penguin Books, $1.25.

Jerome, Judson, *The Poet and the Poem*, Writer's Digest, 1963, $4.50.

Lawler, James R., *An Anthology of French Poetry*, Oxford University Press, 1961.

Leavenworth, Russell E., editor, *Poems From 6 Centuries*, Chandler Publishing Company, 1962, $1.75.

Lewis, Richard, editor, *The Moment of Wonder: A Collection of Chinese and Japanese Poetry*, Dial Press, 1964, $3.95.

Lytle, Ruby, *What is the Moon?* Japanese-Haiku Sequence, Tuttle Publishing Company, 1965, $1.00.

McCloskey, Robert, *Time of Wonder*, Viking Press, 1958, $3.37.

McNeil and Zimmer, editors, *Living Poetry*, Globe Book Company, 1950, $3.84, $2.88.

Rockowitz and Kaplan, *The World of Poetry*, Globe Book Company, 1965, $3.96, $2.97.

Rosenthal, M. L., *The Modern Poets: A Critical Introduction*, Oxford University Press, 1965, $2.25.

Tennyson, Alfred Lord, *The Charge of the Light Brigade*, Golden Press, 1964.

Tennyson and Millay, *Idylls of the King—The King's Henchman*, Noble and Noble, 1965.

Tresselt, Alvin, *Hide and Seek Fog*, Lothrop, Lee and Shepard Company, Inc., 1965, $3.50.

ANNOTATED LIST BY PUBLISHERS

ABINGDON
201 8th AVENUE S., NASHVILLE, TENN.

1. Hunt and Carlson; *Masks and Mask Makers*; 67 p.; 1961; $3.00. Secondary Teacher. Pictures, masks of Americas, Africa, Pacific and Europe with explanation of construction and use. How to make a mask.

2. Olsen, Ib Spang; *The Marsh Crone's Brew*; 1960; $1.50. Grades 4–8. A Danish folktale which explains the mist on the marshes and the changing of the seasons.

HARRY N. ABRAMS, INC.
6 W. 57th STREET, NEW YORK 19, N.Y.

1. Bazin, Germain; *French Impressionist Paintings in the Louvre*; 304 p; 1966; $4.95; Secondary Teacher. 78 pages of text, over 100 full color plates with a page of commentary by the

155

curator-in-chief of the Louvre. Canvas size and list of illustrations by artist.

2. Janson, H. W. and Janson; *The Story of Painting for Young People*; 256 p.; n.d.; Secondary. 245 reproductions, 32 in full color. Chronological treatment from cave paintings to Dali with readable text which interprets art in terms of its time, place and author.

ALLYN AND BACON
150 TREMONT STREET, BOSTON 11, MASS.

CAVALCADE SERIES

A textbook series intended for H.S. which presents wide surveys of literature in English. Illustrated, study aids, biographical sketches. Arranged by form, with introduction. Glossary.

1. Horn, Gunnar; *A Cavalcade of American Writing*; 780 p.; 1966.
2. Horn, Gunnar; *A Cavalcade of British Writing*; 808 p.; 1961.
3. Horn, Gunnar; *A Cavalcade of World Writing*; 713 p.; 1966.
4. Sullivan, Catherine J.; *A Cavalcade of Life in Writing*; 652 p.; 1963.
5. Austin and Mills; *The Sound of Poetry*; 383 p.; 1964; Elementary. Verses chosen to be read *to* young children from Mother Goose to T. S. Elliot, Marianne Moore to Haiku. Eleven broad categories, 385 titles from 399 authors. Ten page introduction and guide.
6. DeMille, A. B.; *Three English Comedies*; 479 p.; 1924–1965; Sr. H.S.–Coll. "*She Stoops to Conquer*", "*The Rivals*", "*The School for Scandal*" with background notes and lives of Goldsmith and Sheridan.
7. McGeary, Jefferson and Fredette; *My World of Art, Books* 1–6; 90 p.; 1963; $2.12, manual $.84; Grades 1–6. Paper, 15″ x 11⅜″ removable pages. Most pages offer background color, a "motivational clue" and are to be used. Photographs and brief text control direction.
8. McGehee and Nelson; *People and Music* (rev.); 409 p.; 1966; H.S. History of music as a part of civilization affecting literature, painting, sculpture. Questions, glossary, book and audio guides. Western and non-western; classical and folk.

AMERICAN BOOK COMPANY
55 5th AVENUE, NEW YORK, N.Y. 10003

1. Guerber, H. A.; *Myths of Greece and Rome*; 427 p.; 1921; $4.75; Elementary and secondary. Myths related with reference to their influence on art and literature.
2. McKinney, Howard D.; *Music and Man*; 409 p.; 1962; Secondary. A general survey of music, both professional and traditional from a view of contemporary American culture.

AMERICAN FOLKLORE SOCIETY
UNIVERSITY OF TEXAS
BOX 7819, UNIVERSITY STATION, AUSTIN, TEXAS 78712

1. Gimbutas, Marija; *Ancient Symbolism in Lithuanian Folk Art*; 148 p.; 1958; $2.50; H.S., College, Teachers. Study of the folk art of Lithuania and its symbolic form and significance as perhaps the longest survivals of prehistoric agriculturists. Pertinent also to all Western culture.

AMERICAN HERITAGE PUBLISHING COMPANY
SIMON AND SCHUSTER, INC.
630 FIFTH AVENUE, NEW YORK, N.Y. 10020

1. Editors of "American Heritage"; *The American Heritage Book of Indians*; 417 p.; 1961; $15.00; Elementary–Secondary. Extensively illustrated (500) examination of the richness and variety of American Indian culture from Pleistocene times to reservations.

2. Editors of "Horizon"; *The Light of the Past*; 288 p.; 1965; $13.95; H.S., College. A treasury of "Horizon" which contains 28 articles on many cultures and times by leading authorities. 315 reproductions, 75 in color.

APPLETON-CENTURY-CROFTS, INCORPORATED
440 PARK AVENUE, SOUTH, NEW YORK, N.Y. 10016

1. Sansom, G. B.; *Japan: A Short Cultural History* (revised); 524 p.; 1962; $5.75; Teacher, College. Originally published in 1931, a chronological treatment of literature, institutions, art lore, religion and thought.

ASSOCIATION PRESS
291 BROADWAY, NEW YORK, N.Y. 10007

1. Macfarlan, Allan A.; *Book of American Indian Games*; 284 p.; 1958; $3.95; Secondary, Teacher. 150 games of American Indians from the Northwest coast to the Atlantic. Diagrams, sketches and supplementary information on each.

2. Rossler, Theodore W.; *Treasury of American Indian Tales*; 310 p.; 1957; $3.95; Elementary–Jr. H.S. 44 Tales from 27 tribes arranged by theme—Adventure, Customs, Character, etc.

BANTAM
271 MADISON AVENUE, NEW YORK, N.Y. 10016

1. Ch'u Chai and Winberg Chai, editors; *The Humanist Way in Ancient China: Essential Works of Confucianism*; 367 p.; 1965; $.95; College. Confucius and his disciples, Mencius, Hsün Tzu, Tung Chung-Shu, presented through their works.

2. Conrad, Joseph; *Three Short Novels*; 206 p.; 1960; $.50; Secondary, College. *Heart of Darkness, Youth* and *Typhoon*.

3. Crane, Milton, editor; *50 Great American Short Stories*; 502 p.; 1965; $.95; Secondary, College. Poe, Harte, Benet, Finley,

Peter Dunne, James Reid Parker, Washington Irving, etc. Classics and little known stories.

4. Crane, Milton, editor; *50 Great Poets*; 591 p.; 1961; $1.25; H.S., College. Over 500 poems by 50 outstanding poets. Includes entire first books of *The Iliad* and *The Aeneid*. As many as twenty works by some poets.

5. Flores, Angel, editor; *Spanish Drama*; 473 p.; 1962; $.75; H.S., College. Plays by Lorca, Benavente, Echegaray, Moratin, Calderon, Alarcón, DeVega, DeMolina, Cervantes and DeRueda.

6. Fowlie, Wallace, editor and translator; *Classical French Drama*; 277 p.; 1962; $.60., College. *The Cid, The Barber of Seville, Phaedra, The Intellectual Ladies* and *The Game of Love and Chance.*

7. Gassner, John, editor; *Four Great Elizabethan Plays*; 316 p.; 1960; $.75; H.S., College. *Doctor Faustus, The Dutchess of Malfi, The Shoemaker's Holiday,* and *Volpone.*

8. Gassner, John, editor; *Medieval and Tudor Drama*; 453 p.; 1963; $1.25; H.S., College. Includes pagan and passion drama, morality play *Everyman, Ralph Roister Doister, Gammer Gurton's Needle, and Gorboduc.* Bibliography.

9. Hanrahan, Gene Z., editor; *50 Great Oriental Stories*; 470 p.; 1965; $.95; Secondary, College. From Japan, China, India, Ceylon, and Southeast Asia.

10. McAndrew, Andrew R., editor; *Four Soviet Masterpieces*; 248 p.; 1965; $.95; H.S., College. Modern Soviet literature. *The Ore* by Vladimov, *I'd Be Honest If They'd Let Me* by Voinovich, *Halfway to the Moon* by Aksenov, and *The Kabiasy Imps* by Kazakov.

11. Twain, Mark; *The Complete Short Stories of Mark Twain;* 679 p.; 1957; $.95; Secondary, College. 60 stories arranged chronologically; taken from the 37 volume Stormfield Edition of Twain's Works published in 1929 by Harper & Bros.

12. Spector, Robert Donald; *Seven Masterpieces of Gothic Horror*; 465 p.; 1963; $.95; H.S., College. *The Castle of Otranto, The Old English Baron, Mistrust, The White Old Maid, The Heir of Mondolfo, The Fall of the House of Usher,* and *Carmilla.*

13. Turgenev, Ivan; *Fathers and Sons*; 207 p.; 1959; $.60; H.S., College. Classic novel in a new translation that treats the 1848 Revolutionary vs. Absolutist period.

14. Van Buitenen, J.A.B., editor; *Tales of Ancient India*; 204 p.; 1959; $.50. H.S., College. Stories written from 300–500 A.D., India's Golden Age.

15. Wilde, Oscar; *Five Plays by Oscar Wilde*; 298 p.; 1961; $.95; H.S., College. *The Importance of Being Earnest, An Ideal*

Husband, A Woman of No Importance, Lady Windemere's Fan, and *Salomé.*

16. Wilder, Thornton; *Three Plays by Thornton Wilder*; 225 p.; 1966; $.75; H.S., College. *Our Town, The Skin of Our Teeth,* and *The Matchmaker.*

BARRE PUBLISHERS
SOUTH STREET, BARRE, MASS. 01005

1. Chang, Isabelle C.; *Chinese Fairy Tales*; 74 p.; $4.95; 1965; Elementary. 26 legends, each with a maxim from Confucius. Illustrated.

BASIC BOOKS, INCORPORATED
404 PARK AVENUE, S., NEW YORK, N.Y. 10016

1. Grigson, Geoffrey; *Poets in Their Pride*; 175 p.; 1964; $4.95; H.S., College, Teachers. Twelve chapters which discuss 12 English poets from 16th–19th centuries, followed by a number of poems by each.

CHARLES A. BENNETT, INCORPORATED
809 W. DETWEILLER DR., PEORIA, ILL. 61614

1. Nicholas and others; *Art for Young America*; 286 p.; 1962; $4.72; Secondary. Aesthetics approach to color, line, composition, and harmony in painting, sculpture, commercial art, architecture and furnishings.

BLAISDELL PUBLISHING COMPANY, INCORPORATED
725 WYMAN STREET, WALTHAM, MASSACHUSETTS 02154

1. Gayley, Charles Mills, editor; *The Classic Myths in English Literature and Art* (rev.); 597 p.; 1939; $6.95; Grades 5–12. A study of classical mythology thru art and literature. Sketches of the figures and history of mythology.

GEORGE BRAZILLER, INCORPORATED
1 PARK AVENUE, NEW YORK, N.Y. 10016

THE CULTURES OF MANKIND SERIES
The volumes in this series survey cultural periods with works of their best poets, painters, sculptors, philosophers, theologians in attempts to feel the pulse and assess the achievements of each. Selections are arranged to reveal the constitution of each culture with notes where necessary.

1. Brantl, Ruth, editor; *Medieval Culture*; 379 p.; 1966; $6.95; H.S., College, Teacher.

2. Mates, J. and Cantelupe, editors; *Renaissance Culture*; 375 p.; 1966; $6.95; H.S., Coll., T.

3. Peckham, Morse, editor; *Romanticism*; 350 p.; 1965; $6.95; H.S., Coll., T.

4. Phelps, Robert, editor; *20th Century Culture*; 381 p.; 1965; $6.95; H.S., Coll., T.

5. Schneider, Isidor, editor; *The Enlightenment*; 377 p.; 1965; $6.95; H.S., Coll., T.
6. Von Hildebrand, Alice, editor; *Greek Culture*; 382 p.; 1966; $6.95; H.S., Coll., T.
7. Weinstein, Leo, editor; *The Age of Reason*; 351 p.; 1965; $6.95; H.S., Coll., T.
8. Wills, Garry, editor; *Roman Culture*; 370 p.; 1966; $6.95; H.S., Coll., T.

GREAT AGES OF WORLD ARCHITECTURE SERIES
A series of 12 books which introduce the length and breadth of man's need to build, written by experts in each field. Text of approximately 50 pages is followed by over 100 photographs, plans and drawings. Bibliography. Text, Secondary, College.
1. Alex, William; *Japanese Architecture*; 122 p.; 1963; $4.95.
2. Branner, Robert; *Gothic Architecture*; 118 p.; 1961; $4.95.
3. Brown, Frank E., *Roman Architecture*; 112 p.; 1962; $4.95.
4. Hoag, John D.; *Western Islamic Architecture*; 122 p.; 1963; $4.95.
5. Lowry, Bates; *Renaissance Architecture*; 120 p.; 1961; $4.95.
6. MacDonald, William; *Early Christian and Byzantine Architecture*; 112 p.; 1962; $4.95.
7. Millon, Henry A.; *Baroque and Rococo Architecture*; 122 p.; 1961; $4.95.
8. Robertson, Donald; *Pre-Columbian Architecture*; 124 p.; 1963; $4.95.
9. Saalman, Howard; *Medieval Architecture*; 121 p.; 1962; $4.95.
10. Scranton, Robert L.; *Greek Architecture*; 118 p.; 1962; $4.95.
11. Scully, Vincent Jr.; *Modern Architecture*; 121 p.; 1961; $4.95.
12. Wu, Nelson I.; *Chinese and Indian Architecture*; 123 p.; 1963; $4.95.

GREAT AMERICAN ARTISTS SERIES
A series of volumes devoted to American artists. 30 pages of text followed by over 80 reproductions, 16 in full color. Chronological notes, Bibliographies. Text, H.S., College.
1. Goodrich, Lloyd; *Albert P. Ryder*; 126 p.; 1959; $4.95.
2. Goossen, E. C.; *Stuart Davis*; 1959; $4.95.
3. Hess, Thomas B.; *Willem De Kooning*; 1959; $4.95.
4. O'Hara, Frank; *Jackson Pollock*; 1959; $4.95.
5. Porter, Fairfield; *Thomas Eakins*; 1959; $4.95.

MASTERS OF WORLD ARCHITECTURE SERIES
An 11 volume series on leading architects of the modern school. Each volume contains 30 pages of text by an expert in the field followed by over 80 pages of photos, drawings and

plans. Bibliography, Chronology. 1960; $4.95 ea. Text, H.S., College.

1. Bush-Brown, Albert; *Louis Sullivan.*
2. Choay, Françoise; *Le Corbusier.*
3. Collins, George R.; *Antonio Gaudí.*
4. Drexler, Arthur; *Ludwig Mies Van Der Rohe.*
5. Fitch, James Marston; *Walter Gropius.*
6. Gutheim, Frederick; *Alvar Aalto.*
7. Huxtable, Ada Louise; *Pier Luigi Nervi.*
8. McCoy, Esther; *Richard Neutra.*
9. Papadaki, Stamo; *Oscar Niemeyer.*
10. Scully, Vincent Jr.; *Frank Lloyd Wright.*
11. Von Eckart, Wolf; *Eric Mendelsohn.*

ADDITIONAL TITLES

1. Harris, Neil; *The Artist in American Society: The Formative Years 1790–1860*; 412 p.; 1966; $7.50; H.S., College, Teachers. "An inquiry into the relationship between a community's values and its culture." Three levels are explored: social attitudes toward visual arts as communal enterprises, the status and ideals of the artists and public image of that role. The Americanization of the American artist.
2. McCoubrey, John W.; *American Tradition in Painting*; 128 p.; 1963; $4.95; H.S., College, Teachers. "What is distinctively American about American painting?" Colonial portraits, landscapes, genre, and ashcan school, all are discussed. 68 black and white reproductions with text reference.

BRUCE PUBLISHING COMPANY
400 N. BROADWAY, MILWAUKEE, WISCONSIN 53201

1. Getlein, Frank and Dorothy; *Christianity in Modern Art*; 227 p.; 1961; $5.00; Advanced H.S., College. Mid-20th-century art in painting, sculpture, architecture and the graphic arts primarily related to the Roman Catholic Church but illustrating universal examples of Christian art.

UNIVERSITY OF CALIFORNIA PRESS
BERKELEY, CALIFORNIA 94720

1. Bagby, Philip; *Culture and History*; 244 p.; 1963; $1.50; Teachers and College. An analysis of nine major civilizations with the techniques of anthropology. An attempt to formulate rules of historical action.

CAXTON PRINTERS, LTD.
CALDWELL, IDAHO 83605

1. O'Donnell, J. E.; *Japanese Folktales*; 92 p.; 1958; $5.00; Grades 4–6 reading level, K–6 interest level. Eight myths, legends, and tales which aim at pointing out the universality of children's feelings.

CHANDLER PUBLISHING COMPANY
124 SPEAR STREET, SAN FRANCISCO, CALIF. 94105

1. Kagan, Pauline Wright; *From Adventure to Experience Through Art*; 76 p.; 1959; $2.25; Teachers. Theories and principles of art related to everyday life in an attempt to aid the teaching of art to children.

2. Leavenworth, Russell E.; *Poems from 6 Centuries*; 309 p.; 1962; $1.75; Secondary, College. An anthology which emphasizes breadth with each poet included, the inclusion of several complete long poems and a familiar body of poetry. Chronological from Chaucer to William Carlos Williams.

COLUMBIA UNIVERSITY PRESS
2960 BROADWAY, NEW YORK, N.Y. 10027

INTRODUCTION TO ORIENTAL CIVILIZATION SERIES

A three volume series within the *Records of Civilization Series*. Paper. Source readings intended to reveal the spiritual and intellectual traditions current in India, Pakistan, Japan, and China. Introductions to sections and selections. In general, the first volume contains selections from the past that remain pertinent today; the second volume contains recent works. 1958; H.S., College.

1. DeBary, William Theodore, editor; *Sources of Chinese Tradition*; (2 vols.)

2. DeBary, William Theodore, editor; *Sources of Indian Tradition*; (2 vols.)

3. DeBary, William Theodore, editor; *Sources of Japanese Tradition*; (2 vols.)

DELL
750 THIRD AVENUE, NEW YORK, N.Y. 10017

FAMOUS AMERICAN PLAYS SERIES

1. Clurman, Harold, editor; *Famous American Plays of the 1930's*; 480 p.; 1959; $.75. *The Time of Your Life, Idiot's Delight, Of Mice and Men, Awake and Sing, End of Summer.*

2. Hewes, Henry, editor; *Famous American Plays of the 1940's*; 447 p.; 1960; $.75. *Skin of Our Teeth, Home of the Brave, All My Sons, Lost in the Stars,* and *Member of the Wedding.*

3. McGowan, Kenneth, editor; *Famous American Plays of the 1920's*; 509 p.; 1959; $.75. *Moon of the Caribbees, What Price Glory?, They Knew What They Wanted, Porgy, Street Scene,* and *Holiday.*

4. Strasberg, Lee, editor; *Famous American plays of the 1950's*; 415 p.; 1962; $.75. *Camino Réal, The Autumn Garden, Tea and Sympathy, The Zoo Story, A Hatful of Rain.*

GREAT SHORT STORIES SERIES
A series of anthologies with introduction, from all ages, traditional and literary origin.

1. Bellow, Saul, editor; *Great Jewish Short Stories*; 414 p.; 1963; $.50.
2. Mercier, Vivian, editor; *Great Irish Short Stories*; 384 p.; 1964; $.60.
3. Pasinetti, P. M., editor; *Great Italian Short Stories*; 412 p.; 1959; $.60.
4. Spender, Stephen, editor; *Great German Short Stories;* 284 p.; 1960; $.50.
5. Reeve, F. D., editor; *Great Soviet Short Stories*; 480 p.; 1962; $.75.

ADDITIONAL TITLES

1. Brinnin, John Malcolm, ed.; *Emily Dickinson*; 160 p.; 1960; $.35; H.S., Coll. One in the series which includes the works of a single poet with an introduction, chronology, bibliography, and notes on the poems.
2. Chekhov, O'Casey, Miller, Ibsen, Shaw, Williams; *Six Great Modern Plays*; 512 p.; 1956; $.75; H.S., Coll.; *The Master Builder, Mrs. Warren's Profession, The Three Sisters, Red Roses for Me, The Glass Menagerie,* and *All My Sons.*
3. Corrigan, Robert W., ed.; *The Twentieth Century*; 511 p.; $.95; H.S., Coll.; Shaw—*Heartbreak House,* Galsworthy—*Loyalties,* Coward—*Private Lives,* Bagnold—*The Chalk Garden,* Bolt— *A Man for All Seasons,* and *Jellico—The Knack.*
4. Cottrell, Leonard; *The Horizon Book of Lost Worlds*; 383 p.; 1962; $.75; H.S., Coll. Nine ancient civilizations depicted through the discoveries of archaeology; how the people lived, their beliefs, art, literature, etc.
5. Drew, Elizabeth; *The Novel: A Modern Guide to 15 English Masterpieces*; 287 p.; 1963; $.60; H.S., Coll.; *Moll Flanders, Clarissa, Tom Jones, Lord Jim, Vanity Fair, Emma, The Mill on the Floss, Tristram Shandy, Far from the Maddening Crowd, Wuthering Heights, Portrait of the Artist as a Young Man, Women in Love, Portrait of a Lady, To the Lighthouse,* and *Great Expectations* treated separately.
6. Drew, Elizabeth; *Poetry: A Modern Guide to Its Understanding and Enjoyment*; 287 p.; 1959; $.50; H.S., Coll. The techniques of Poetry: language, symbolism, and rhythms plus its themes: time, death, nature, love, etc. with extensive illustration.
7. Feldmann, Susan, ed.; *African Myths and Tales*; 318 p.; 1963; $.50; Elem.–Coll. Myths and tales arranged separately as creation myths, trickster tales, explanatory tales or legends, fables and adventure tales.
8. Feldman, Susan, ed.; *The Story Telling Stone: Myths and Tales of the American Indians*; 271 p.; 1965; $.60; Elem.–Coll. Fifty-

two tales arranged as creation myths, trickster tales, hero and magic tales, from many sources. Introduction, Bibliography.

9. Flores, Angel, ed.; *Medieval Age*; 606 p.; 1963; $.95; H.S., Coll. Includes *The Lay of the Nibelunge, The Cid, Song of Roland, Beowulf*, with lyric, prose, fiction works by Dante, Chaucer, and Villon.

10. Houghton, Norris, ed.; *Great Russian Plays*; 511 p.; 1960; $.75; H.S., Coll. *The Inspector General, A Month in the Country, The Power of Darkness, The Cherry Orchard, He Who Gets Slapped*, and *The Lower Depths*.

11. Houghton, Norris, ed.; *The Romantic Influence*; 543 p.; 1963; $.95; H.S., Coll. Goethe's *Faust*, Part I; Schiller's *Mary Stuart*, Hugo's *Hernani*, and Rostand's *Cyrano*.

12. Houghton, Norris, ed.; *Seeds of Modern Drama*; 413 p.; 1963; $.75; H.S., Coll.; Zola's *Thérèse Raquin*, Ibsen's *An Enemy of the People*, Hauptmann's *The Weavers*, Strindberg's *Miss Julie*, and Chekhov's *The Sea Gull*.

13. Hunter, Sam; *Modern American Painting and Sculpture*; 256 p.; $.95; 1959; Bellows and Eaking to Pollock and DeKooning. Twenty-four color reproductions, 24 black and white.

14. Hunter, Sam; *Modern French Painting: Fifty Artists from Manet to Picasso*; 256 p.; 1956; $.95; H.S. Twenty-four color plates, 24 black and white plates, chronology, glossary. A chronological approach.

15. Kazin, Alfred, and Aaron, eds.; *Emerson, a Modern Anthology*; 383 p.; 1958; $.50; H.S., Coll. The essence of Emerson, arranged in themes such as *Morning, Noon and Night, Our Abused Age, The Great Man, Art and Artists*, and *The World in Brief*.

16. McDermott, John Francis; *The World of Washington Irving*; 320 p.; 1965; $.50; H.S., Coll. Selections from *The Alhambra, A Tour of the Prairies, A History of New York, Tales of a Traveler, The Sketchbook*, and *Bracebridge Hall*.

17. Mertz, Barbara; *Temples, Tombs and Hieroglyphs: the Story of Egyptology*; 347 p.; 1964; $1.95; H.S., Coll. The history and culture of Egypt as revealed by archaeology.

18. Proust, Marcel; *Marcel Proust on Art and Literature: 1896–1919*; 416 p.; 1964; $2.25; H.S., Coll. The best of Proust in essays and comments on the problems of artistic contemplation, the aesthetic faith, the nature of taste as well as impressions of Watteau, Rembrandt, Monet, Geothe, Stendahl, Tolstoy and Dostoyevsky.

19. Seuphor, Michael; *Abstract Painting*; 192 p.; 1964; $.95; H.S., Coll. *Fifty Years of Accomplishment, from Kandinsky to the*

Present. Extensive black-and-white and color illustrations, authoritative text.

20. Turgenev, Tolstoy, Dostoyevsky, and Chekhov; *Four Great Russian Short Novels*; 383 p.; 1959; $.50; H.S, Coll. *First Love, Master and Man, The Gambler,* and *The Duel.*

21. Warren, Robert Penn and Erskine, eds.; *Short Story Masterpieces*; 542 p.; 1954; $.75; H.S., Coll. Thirty-six stories by Aiken, Conrad, Crane, Faulkner, Fitzgerald, Hemingway, Joyce, Lardner, Lawrence, Lewis, Salinger, Thurber, O'Faolain and others.

THE DIAL PRESS
750 THIRD AVE., NEW YORK, N.Y. 10017

1. Jennings, Gary; *Black Magic, White Magic*; 160 p.; 1964; $3.75; Elem., Jr. H.S. The place of magic in man's story: alchemy, curing, soothsaying, ghosts and witches, "Little People", superstition or today's magic are explained in a simplified manner.

2. Lewis, Rich, ed.; *The Moment of Wonder, A Collection of Chinese and Japanese Poetry*; 134 p.; 1964; $3.95; All. A collection including haiku, of children's poems from all ages, illustrated with paintings by Chinese and Japanese masters.

DODD, MEAD AND CO.
432 PARK AVE. S., NEW YORK, N.Y. 10016

1. Bergere, Thea and Richard; *From Stones to Skyscrapers*; 84 p.; 1960; $3.50; Upper Elem., Jr. H.S.; The story of man's architecture from prehistoric structures to 1960 in clear text, necessarily condensed. Over 100 drawings illustrate major architectural styles and features. Glossary.

2. Buell, Hal; *Festivals of Japan*; 79 p.; 1965; $2.99; Elem. Photographs with text which show the practices surrounding major festivals. Origins are discussed.

3. Eells, Elsie Spicer; *Tales from the Amazon*; 243 p.; 1965; $3.00; Elem., Jr. H.S. Twenty tales from South America—myths, legends, humorous tales that reveal culture.

4. Hughes, Langston and Bontemps, eds.; *The Book of Negro Folklore*; 624 p.; 1966; $6.50; All. The lore of the ante and post bellum American Negro in tales, rhymes, memoirs, ghost tales, magic, sermons, spirituals, ballads, blues, streetcries, verse, etc.

5. Joyce, James; *The Cat and the Devil*; 1964; $3.50; Elem. A French fable adapted by James Joyce for his grandson—illustrations notable.

DOVER PUBLICATIONS INC.
180 VARICK ST., NEW YORK, N.Y. 10014

1. Jackson, George Pullen, ed.; *Spiritual Folk Songs of Early America*; 254 p.; 1964; $2.00; H.S., Coll. Paper edition of the 1937

volume which surveys the song-book and sacred harp era of 1800–1875. 250 songs, each with text, background and analysis. The standard work on a tradition which still exists.

2. Santayana, George; *The Sense of Beauty*; 168 p.; 1955; $1.00; Adv. H.S., Coll., T. A reprint of the classic first published in 1896. Considers the conditions, causes and relation to man's feelings of beauty. The beauty of form.

3. Segy, Ladislas; *African Sculpture*; 244 p.; 1958; $2.00; All. Covers 50 art-producing tribes of west and central Africa. Thirty-four page introduction and analysis of content and expression followed by 164 full-page plates.

FARRAR, STRAUSS AND GIROUX
19 UNION SQUARE, W., NEW YORK, N.Y. 10003

1. MacManus, Seumas; *The Bold Heroes or Hungry Hill and Other Irish Folk Tales*; 207 p.; 1951; $2.95; Elem., H.S. Twelve tales retold by one of Ireland's leading tellers of tales or shanachies.

FLEET PUBLISHING CORP.
230 PARK AVE., NEW YORK, N.Y. 10017

1. Dobler, Lavinia; *Customs and Holidays Around the World*; 185 p.; 1962; $4.50; Elem., H.S. A seasonal approach to celebrations and festivals with emphasis on current practice and national comparisons.

FUNK AND WAGNALLS
360 LEXINGTON AVE., NEW YORK, N.Y. 10017

1. Bryant, Margaret M.; *Current American Usage*; 239 p.; 1962; $5.00; H.S., Coll., T. Survey of American speech habits from numerous sources. Regional analysis is based upon the linguistic atlas. Three usage levels and substandard glossary, map, evidence analysis of five linguistic studies for selected entries.

2. Leach, Maria; *The Beginning: Myths Around the World*; 243 p.; 1956; $3.75; Upper Elem., H.S., T. American Indian, Oceanic, Siberian, Classic myths told simply but with authenticity. Bibliography and introduction with motif analysis.

GARRARD PUBLISHING CO.
2 OVERHILL RD., SCARSDALE, N.Y. 10583

FOLKLORE OF THE WORLD SERIES; Edward W. Dolch

1. *Stories from Alaska*; 167 p.; 1961; $2.49; Animal tales and legends of the Indian and Eskimo.

2. *Stories from Canada*; 167 p.; $2.49; French, Indian, Eskimo and English myths, munchausen and legends.

3. *Stories from France*; 165 p.; 1963; $2.49; Animal tales, legends.

4. *Stories from Hawaii*; 167 p.; 1960; $2.49; 3–4 reading; K–4 interest. Tales retold in simple language, large type, illustrated. Special

word glossary. Legends, myths, and tales.

5. *Stories from India*; 165 p.; 1961; $2.49; Mythology, animal tales, legends.

6. *Stories from Italy*; 167 p.; 1962; $2.49; Deals with legends of folk, church, and court.

7. *Stories from Japan*; 167 p.; 1960; $2.49; Legends and tales of classical and medieval Japan.

8. *Stories from Mexico*; 167 p.; 1960; $2.49; Animal tales and legends from old Mexico and the Aztecs.

9. *Stories from Old China*; 166 p.; 1964; $2.49; Legends and tales from classical China.

10. *Stories from Old Egypt*; 167 p.; 1964; $2.49; Myths, tales and legends of ancient Egypt.

11. *Stories from Old Russia*; 167 p.; 1964; $2.49; 3–4 reading; K–4 interest. Tales of Tsarist Russia.

12. *Stories from Spain*; 167 p.; 1962; $2.49; Moorish and Spanish tales and legends.

GINN AND CO.
STATLER BLDG., BACK BAY P.O. 191, BOSTON, MASS. 02117

1. Fraenkel, Gerd; *What is Language?*; 60 p.; 1965; H.S. A paperbound study of language as speech—central ideas and concepts to the place of language in our lives.

2. Pannwitt, Barbara, ed.; *The Art of Short Fiction*; 475 p.; 1964; H.S., Coll. A humanistic approach to short fiction in terms of its artistic expression; stories by leading writers (with introductions) with their humanistic themes.

3. Pflug, Raymond J.; *The Adventures of Huckleberry Finn: Evolution of a Classic*; 67 p.; H.S.; Primary source material tracing the growth of Huckleberry Finn's popularity with exercises in reaction for the students. Designed as a preparation for longer critical papers.

4. Shanker, Sidney; *Semantics: The Magic of Words*; 122 p.; 1965; H.S., Coll. Investigation into the relatedness of language with differences and similarities occurring from change. Questions, word list.

5. West, William W., ed.; *On Writing, by Writers*; 403 p.; 1966; H.S., Coll. Explanation of the mechanics of literature in an attempt to encourage understanding and appreciation of the content. Poetry to technical writing by outstanding modern writers. Includes introductions and selections with author commentary for each chapter.

GLOBE BOOK CO.
175 FIFTH AVE., NEW YORK, N.Y. 10010

1. Goodman, Roger B.; *World-Wide Short Stories*; 352 p.; 1966; $2.25; H.S. Brief history of the short story plus 40 short stories

from many lands grouped into six themes such as: man makes war, man weighs points of view, man explores the unknown, etc. Teacher guide and questions, introduction to each story.

2. Holder, and others, eds.; *Journeys in American Literature*; 722 p.; 1958; $4.36; H.S. Textbook which presents classic pieces of prose and poetry in a chronological unit arrangement. Includes news writing, biography and autobiography, drama, short story and novel as well as folklore. Teacher guide, text questions.

3. Konick, Marcus; *Six Complete World Plays and a History of World Drama*; 689 p.; 1963; $3.96; H.S. *Antigone, Cyrano, Cherry Orchard, Enemy of the People, Caesar and Cleopatra,* and *Everyman.* Introduction, questions, production notes for each play. Teacher's guide.

4. McNeil and Zimmer, eds.; *Living Poetry*; 478 p.; 1950; $3.84; H.S. Poems grouped into themes such as modern civilization, the city, looking at life, people, the sea, war, love of country, etc. With a brief guide to poetry and glossary.

5. Popp, Lilian M.; *Four Complete Heritage Novels*; 605 p.; 1963; $4.20; H.S. *Wilderness Clearing, Banners at Shenandoah, Red Pony, A Walk in the Sun.* Notes on each author and novel, questions, vocabularly, activties and teacher's guide.

6. Popp, Lilian M.; *Four Complete Modern Novels*; 709 p.; 1962; $4.20; H.S. *Teahouse of the August Moon, Romance of Rosy Ridge, Sea of Grass, Wreck of the Mary Deare.* Notes, questions, and teacher's guide.

7. Popp, Lilian M.; *Four Complete Novels of Character and Courage;* 644 p.; 1964; $4.20; H.S. *Silas Marner, Enchanted Voyage, Good Morning Miss Dove,* and *Bridge over the River Kwai.* Notes, questions, and teacher's guide.

8. Rockowitz and Kaplan; *The World of Poetry*; 584 p.; 1965; $3.96; H.S. 500 poems grouped into 37 categories and indexed also by chronology. Questions and teacher's guide which suggests curriculum and approach.

9. Shapiro, Alan; *American Literature; Four Representative Types;* 500 p.; 1964; $4.20; H.S. The Novel: *April Morning,* The Drama: *The Andersonville Trial,* The True Narrative: *Hiroshima,* and The Biography: *Eleanor Roosevelt.* Commentary, questions, and teacher's guide.

10. Sneratsky, R. and Reilly, eds.; *The Lively Arts: Four Representative Types;* 236 p.; 1964; $4.20; H.S., Novel: *The African Queen,* The Stage Play: *Inherit the Wind,* Television Script: *Abraham Lincoln—the early Years,* and The Screenplay: *Marty.* Notes, author sketch, teacher's guide, reviews. Novel also includes excerpts from film script.

THE GOLDEN PRESS, INC.
850 THIRD AVE., NEW YORK, N.Y. 10022

1. The Editors of "Life"; *The World's Great Religions*; 189 p.; 1958; grades 4–8. Young readers edition which includes color reproductions and photographs with text explanatory of major living religions.

2. Munro, Eleanor C.; *The Encyclopedia of Art*; 299 p.; 1961; $9.95; Elem. and up. "Painting and sculpture, architecture and ornament, from prehistoric times to the twentieth century." Over 650 plates (300 color) Glossaries of artists and art terms, text places art in context.

3. Tennyson, Alfred Lord; *The Charge of The Light Brigade*; 1964; All. Full and double page illustrations are coupled with Tennyson's poem to capture the rigidity, fervor and heroism of the historical event.

4. White, Anne Terry; *The Golden Treasury of Myths and Legends*; 164 p.; 1959; grades 4–8. Seventeen Legends and Myths adapted: Greek, Roman, Viking, Celtic, Persian and French. Introduction explains the oral form and backgrounds. Original illustrations.

GROSSETT AND DUNLAP, INC.
51 MADISON AVE., NEW YORK, N.Y. 10010

1. Ames, Russell; *The Story of American Folk Song*; 276 p.; 1960; Elem., H.S. A chronological and thematic treatment of the songs and ballads contained in American history. Verses and versions are included with contextual material.

2. Funk, Wilfred; *Word Origins and Their Romantic Stories*; 432 p.; 1950; Ref.; Elem., H.S. Words and origins are grouped by topic such as business terms, war, science, eating, gardening terms, and sources for attitude and emotion words, etc.

THE GROVE PRESS, INC.
80 UNIVERSITY PL., NEW YORK, N.Y. 10003

1. Allen, Donald M., ed.; *The New American Poetry*; 452 p.; 1960; $2.95; H.S., Coll. An anthology of 215 poems by 44 poets, biographical notes, bibliog. and preface background. Post W.W. II. Also a section of statements on poetics by 15 poets.

2. Jahn, Janheinz; *Muntu: The New African Culture*; 267 p.; 1961; $2.45; Adv. H.S., Coll., T. Consideration of traditions and new African thought in religion, language, philosophy, literature, art, music, and dance. Bibliog., illustrations, maps.

3. Keene, Donald; *Japanese Literature: An Introduction for Western Readers*; 114 p.; 1945; $1.45; Adv. H.S., Coll. An authoritative account of Japanese literature which considers separately: poetry, theater, the novel and Western influence. Bibliog.

4. Moon, Samuel, ed.; *One Act: Eleven Short Plays of the Modern*

169

Theater; 370 p.; 1961; $1.95; H.S., Coll. Plays by Strindberg and Pirandello, Saroyan, Miller, Williams, Yeats, MacLeisch, Inesco, Wilder, O'Casey and Anouilh.

5. Paz, Octavio; *The Labyrinth of Solitude: Life and Thought in Mexico*; 212 p.; 1961; $1.95; H.S., Coll. A study of Mexican culture by a poet who is also essayist, playwright, editor and diplomat.

6. White, Leslie A.; *The Science of Culture*; 44 p.; 1949; $2.95; Adv. H.S., Coll. A classic study of man's relation to his culture and the science of "culturology". Symbols, psychology, tools, mind, energy and civilization are all central to this exploration of man.

HASTINGS HOUSE PUBLISHERS, INC.
101 E. 50th ST., NEW YORK, N.Y. 10022

1. Cooney, Barbara; *The Little Juggler*; 46 p.; 1961; $3.25; Elem. An adaptation of the French legend of the juggler of Notre Dame based upon the 13th century manuscript and research. Extensively illustrated.

HEATH, D. C. AND CO.
285 COLUMBUS AVE., BOSTON, MASS. 02116

1. Hook, J. N.; *Writing Creatively*; 305 p.; 1963; H.S. Text covering expository writing as well as fiction, poetry and drama. Principles of writing and the craft of the professional.

HILL AND WANG, INC.
141 5th AVE., NEW YORK, N.Y. 10010

1. Brown, Ivor; *How Shakespeare Spent the Day*; 237 p.; 1963; $5.00; H.S., Coll. A study of Shakespeare as playwright, investor, manager and actor in the workaday world. An attempt to see a versatile genius at his job.

2. Frenz, Horst, ed.; *American Playwrights on Drama*; 174 p.; 1965; $3.95; H.S., Coll. Essays, notes, etc. by 14 playwrights, includes O'Neill, Anderson, Wilder, Williams, Miller, Green, Inge, Jeffers, Behrman, Rice, MacLeish, Hansberry, Albee, Lawson.

3. Geismar, Maxwell, ed.; *Jack London, Short Stories*; 228 p.; 1960; $1.75; H.S., Coll. Eighteen of London's later stories including *To Build a Fire* and *Love of Life* chosen for excellence and variety.

HOUGHTON MIFFLIN CO.
2 PARK ST., BOSTON, MASS. 02107

1. Chase, Jewett, and Evans, eds.; *Values in Literature*; 649 p.; 1965; H.S. A textbook aimed at grade 9 which groups classic prose and poetry into such themes as suspense, insights, people, imagery, moments of wonder, etc. Also treats forms such as

170

poetry, the novel, and short story. Questions, glossary, teacher's edition and handbook.

2. Twain, Mark; *The Adventures of Tom Sawyer*; 210 p.; 1962; grades 5–8. A duraflex edition, based upon the first American edition. Introductory sketch of Twain and Hannibal. Reading and discussion questions. Available also in hardcover and paper.

KNOPF, ALFRED A. INC.
501 MADISON AVE., NEW YORK, N.Y. 10022

1. Blake, Peter; *The Master Builders*; 399 p.; 1966; $8.00; H.S., Coll. T. Modern architecture through the lives and works of LeCorbusier, Mies van der Rohe, and Frank Lloyd Wright. Very readable text with 134 photos and drawings.

2. Covarrubias, Miguel; *The Eagle, the Jaguar, and the Serpent: Indian Art of the Americas*; 296 p.; 1954; $15.00; H.S., Coll. An introductory section on periods and origins of Eskimo-Indian art and the technique and aesthetics of each of 13 art forms is followed by examination of areas: arctic, N. W. coast, far west, southwest, eastern woodlands, and plains. Illustrated with 112 line drawings, 12 color plates and 100 photos. Extensive bibliography.

LAIDLOW BROS.
THATCHER AND MADISON AVES., RIVER FOREST, ILL. 60305

1. Habberton, Roth and Spears; *World History and Cultures: The Story of Man's Achievements*; 712 p.; 1966; H.S. A world history text with emphasis on cultural achievements. Illustrations of art and architecture.

LITTLE, BROWN & CO.
45 BEACON ST., BOSTON, MASS. 02106

1. Burchard, J. and Bush-Brown; *The Architecture of America* (abridged); 450 p.; 1966; $3.95; H.S., Coll. History and discussions of American architecture, from 1860–1960 except for the first chapter which covers the first 200 years .

2. Davis, Russell, and Ashabranner; *The Lion's Whiskers*; 191 p.; 1959; $3.95; grades 4–8. Forty-one tales from the highlands of Ethiopia retold by their field collectors, educators in charge of producing elementary textbooks. Grouped by tribe.

LOTHROP, LEE, AND SHEPARD CO.
419 PARK AVE. S., NEW YORK, N.Y. 10016

1. Teresselt, Alvin; *Hide and Seek Fog*; 1965; $3.50; K–3. A union of picture and verse-like prose to tell the story of a three-day fog in a Cape Cod village.

McKAY, DAVID CO., INC.
750 THIRD AVE., NEW YORK, N.Y. 10017

1. Cothran, Jean, ed.; *The Magic Calabash; Folk Tales from America's Islands and Alaska;* 88 p.; $2.95; grades 4–8. Sixteen tales from Alaska, Hawaii, Puerto Rico and the Virgin Islands retold from authentic sources with a short explanation of the background of each location.

MacRAE SMITH COMPANY
225 S. 15th ST., PHILADELPHIA, PA. 19102

1. Forsee, Alyesa; *Frank Lloyd Wright: Rebel in Concrete;* 181 p.; 1959; $4.95; H.S. Biography of Frank Lloyd Wright with 20 pages of photographs.

MERRILL, CHARLES E., BOOKS INC., COLLEGE DIVISION
1300 ALUM CREEK DRIVE., COLUMBUS, OHIO 43216

PRANG YOUNG ARTISTS SERIES; Maxcy, Kysar, and Roberson
1. Books 1–8; 30–40 p. each book; 1959; $1.12; grades 1–8; Paper art texts which utilize reproductions, sketches and photographs with grade level text to promote creative expression. Teacher's manual $1.12.

TOLD-AGAIN TALES FROM MANY LANDS
1. Holl, Adelaide; *Magic Tales;* 128 p.; 1964; $2.64; grades 1–4. A series of three supplementary readers containing retellings of legends, fairy tales and little and well known marchen. Extensive two-color illustrations, primary type.
2. Potter and Harley; *First Fairy Tales;* grades 1–2.
3. Potter and Gilbert; *Giants and Fairies;* grades 2–3.

TREASURY OF LITERATURE SERIES;
Jacobs, Johnson and Turner, eds.
1. *Seesaw;* 1966; $2.20; primer. Elementary reading series which contains a large proportion of traditional verse and prose.
2. *Merry-Go-Round;* $2.72; grade 1.
3. *Happiness Hill;* $2.96; grade 2.
4. *Treat Shop;* $3.12; grade 3.
5. *Magic Carpet;* $3.28; grade 4.
6. *Enchanted Isles;* $3.40; grade 5.
7. *Adventure Lands;* $3.52; grade 6.

THE METROPOLITAN MUSEUM OF ART
N.Y. GRAPHIC SOCIETY
5th AVE. AND 82nd ST., NEW YORK, N.Y. 10028

1. Geldzahler, Henry; *American Painting in the Twentieth Century;* 230 p.; 1965; $7.50; H.S. "A concise study of the traditions and innovations in American painting since the turn of the century." Ninety painters are discussed, 155 reproductions (nearly all from the collection of the Metropolitan).

2. McKendry, John J., ed.; *Aesop: Five Centuries of Illustrated Fables*; 90 p.; 1964; $4.95; Elem.–H.S. Forty fables in translations and illustrations ranging from medieval times to the present.

MORROW, WILLIAM & CO.
425 PARK AVE. S., NEW YORK, N.Y. 10016

1. DeOsma, Lupe; *The Witches' Ride and Other Tales from Costa Rica*; 190 p.; 1957; $3.00; Elem. Twelve folk tales retold in English and illustrated with author explanation of the original tales, additions as well as comment on each tale as a variant or indigenous story.
2. Hofsinde, Robert; *Indian Sign Language*; 96 p.; 1956; $2.75; Elem.–Jr. H.S. A handbook containing illustration and explanation for over 500 words in Indian sign language.
3. Kettlekamp, Larry; *Drums, Rattles and Bells*; 47 p.; 1960; Elem. An introduction to percussion instruments in four sections—rattles, drums, keyboard percussion and bells. Primitive and concept forms as well as instructions for constructing several examples are given. Illustrated.

MUSEUM OF MODERN ART
11 W. 53rd ST., NEW YORK, N.Y. 10019

1. Hitchcock, Henry-Russell; *Latin American Architecture Since 1945*; 204 p.; 1955; $6.50; 272 plates illustrate a survey of 46 buildings in 10 countries and Puerto Rico, by a score of architects. Public housing projects and university cities included.

MUSEUM OF PRIMITIVE ART
15 W. 54th ST., NEW YORK, N.Y. 10019

1. Goldwater, Robert; *Senufo Sculpture from West Africa*; 1964; $8.95; H.S., Coll. Examination of an extremely rich and varied African style. Masks, headpieces, figures, staffs, doors, and their place in Senufo Society. 186 illustrations and photographs.
2. Goldwater, Robert; *Traditional Art of the African Nations in the Museum of Primitive Art*; 1961; $6.00; H.S., Coll. The variety of sculpture from 16 independent nations in Africa. Most of the 79 objects illustrated are less than 150 years old but portray the traditional tribal culture.

NATIONAL COUNCIL OF TEACHERS OF ENGLISH
508 S. 6th ST., CHAMPAIGN, ILL. 61810

1. Arnstein, Flora J.; *Poetry in the Elementary Classroom*; 124 p.; 1962; $2.95; T. Consideration of climate and methods for instilling in children a sensitivity for verse.
2. Leary, Lewis, ed.; *The Teacher and American Literature*; 189 p.;

1965; $2.25; T. Papers from the 1964 NCTE convention which deal with literature, its criticism and implications for schools. Sections deal with the novel, Emerson, elementary education.
3. Malmstrom, Jean and Ashley; *Dialects U.S.A.*; 59 p.; 1963; $2.25; H.S., Coll. An introduction to dialect patterns in the U.S. for use in secondary schools. Includes a list of literary selections which illustrate dialects. Bibliography.

THE NATIONAL PRESS
850 HANSEN WAY, PALO ALTO, CALIF. 04304

1. Buker, Alden; *A Humanistic Approach to Music Appreciation*; 200 p.; 1964; H.S., Coll. The role of music in society divided into: music and environment, nations, stage, church, the concert hall, the modern mind. Sample problems. Bibliog.
2. Buker, Alden; *A Social Approach to Music Appreciation*; 90 p.; 1963; H.S., Coll. The place of music in world history from prehistoric and primitive man to electronic music in terse form.

NELSON, THOMAS & SONS
COPEWOOD AND DAVIS STS., CAMDEN, N.J. 08103

1. DeLeeuw, A.; *Indonesian Legends and Folktales*; 160 p.; 1961; grades 5-8. Twenty-six legends and tales from Java, Borneo, Sumatra and Burma. Includes animal tales, mythology, legends retold and drawn from a variety of sources.
2. Mendelsohn, Jack; *God, Allah and Juju—Religion in Africa Today*; 238 p.; 1962; $3.75; H.S., Coll. Africa today in terms of three religious streams. A prominent American Unitarian clergyman investigates attitudes and practices of these in relation to independent Africa.

NEW AMERICAN LIBRARY, INC.
1301 AVE. OF THE AMERICAS, NEW YORK, N.Y. 10019

1. Dean, Vera Micheles; *The Nature of the Non-Western World*; 384 p.; 1966; $.75; H.S., Coll. Based upon introductory course in non-western civilization at the University of Rochester, 1954–1962. Includes Latin America, Africa as well as Asia and the Middle East in a consideration of the many problems facing these areas today and the inherent cultural factors.

NEW YORK GRAPHIC SOCIETY PUBLISHERS, LTD.
140 GREENWICH AVE., GREENWICH, CONN. 06830

MAN THRU HIS ART SERIES; DeSilva, A. and O. von Simson
1. Vol. 1; *War and Peace*; 64 p.; 1964; $7.95; H.S., Coll. How man has reacted throughout the ages to the concepts of war and peace as shown in the art of many cultures. Sixteen color plates, four black and white. Text accompanies each illustration.

174

2. Vol. 2; *Music*; 64 p.; 1964; $7.95; H.S., Coll. Masterpieces and commentary explanatory of the role played by music in many cultures.
3. Vol. 3; *Man and Animal*; 64 p.; 1965; $7.95; H.S., Coll. Twenty studies of artistic expression on man's relationship with the animal throughout prehistory and historic times.

ADDITIONAL TITLES:
1. Baur, John I. H., ed.; *New Art in America*; 280 p.; 1957; $22.50; H.S., Coll. The work of 50 leading painters of the twentieth century. Fifty color plates, 177 black and white illustrations with text by five leading art experts. An attempt to show those artists who formed American art of the period.
2. Bloch, Raymond; *Etruscan Art*; 100 p.; 1965; $10.00; H.S., Coll., T. 56 pages of text, 48 color plates plus black and white illustrations; covers architecture, sculpture, painting and "lesser arts" in an interpretation of the place of art in the Etruscan culture.
3. Cottrell, Leonard; *Realms of Gold*; 269 p.; 1963; $5.95; H.S. The story of the discovery of the Mycenaean civilization and the facts and theories behind the Homeric epic and Greek mythology.
4. Cottrell, Leonard; *The Secrets of Tutankhamen's Tomb*; 135 p.; 1964; $4.50; H.S. The story of the excavation of Tutankhamen's tomb with drawings, photographs and description of its contents and their functions.
5. Dockstader, Frederick J.; *Indian Art in America: The Arts and Crafts of The North American Indian*; 1962; $25.00; 4–Coll., T. 48-page text, 248 items (70 color, 180 black and white). The most comprehensive work on the visual arts of the Indian from Eskimo to Pueblo both prehistoric and historic.
6. Dover, Cedric; *American Negro Art*; 180 p.; 1960; $12.00; H.S., Coll. Eight color plates, 400 halftone reproductions which deal with the backgrounds of American Negro art, its theme, craft expression and current works. Text by an anthropologist long acquainted with this.
7. Kuh, Katherine; *Break-up: the Core of Modern Art*; 132 p.; 1965; $7.95; H.S., Coll. "Deliberately condensed and always accompanied by visual evidence, the text examines works of art with only two objectives: to uncover meanings and motivations." A characteristic of this art is fragmentation.
8. The Museum of Primitive Art; *Masterpieces in the Museum of Primitive Art*; 134 p.; 1965; $4.95; H.S., Coll., T. Primitive art from Africa, Oceania, North America, Mexico, Central and South America and Peru. With short introduction to each section and description of each of the 134 objects. Black and white.

175

9. Newton, Eric; *The Arts of Man*; 315 p.; 1960; $5.95; H.S. 174 examples of art in its widest sense reproduced and examined by a noted critic. Includes ceramics, mosaics, illuminations, coins, glass as well as more conventional media. Covers all periods and cultures.

10. Silverberg, Robert; *The Old Ones: Indians of the American Southwest*; 252 p.; 1965; $4.95; H.S. The story of the Pueblo Indians. Photographs, lists of today's sites, bibliog. Culture is described in the historical frame.

NOBLE & NOBLE, PUBLISHERS INC.
750 THIRD AVE., NEW YORK, N.Y. 10017

COMPARATIVE CLASSICS SERIES

Cloth editions which pair an unabridged classic with a modern work with similar plot or theme. Illustrated from stage and film, study and comparison selections. H.S.

1. Cooke, Olivia M., ed.; *Comparative Poetry: Present and Past*; 1965.

2. Defoe, Trumbull and Coleridge; *Robinson Crusoe, The Raft, The Rhyme of the Ancient Mariner*; 1965.

3. Dickens and Steinbeck; *A Tale of Two Cities, The Moon Is Down*; 1965.

4. Eliot, and Steinbeck; *Silas Marner; The Pearl*; 451 p., 1965.

5. Keyes, Rowena, ed.; *Comparative Classics, Present and Past*; 1953; contains dramas by Goldsmith, Sheridan, Beach and Barry.

6. Read, Warren W., ed.; *Comparative Essays: Present and Past*; 1965.

7. Shakespeare, William, and Anderson; *Julius Caesar* and *Elizabeth the Queen*; 337 p.; 1958.

8. Shakespeare, William, and Balderson; *A Midsummer Night's Dream* and *Berkeley Square*; 1963.

9. Shakespeare, William, and O'Neill; *MacBeth* and *The Emperor Jones*; 1965.

10. Shakespeare, William, and Rostand; *Romeo and Juliet* and *Cyrano De Bergerac*; 1965.

11. Shakespeare, William, and Sophocles and O'Neill; *Hamlet* and *Electra* and *Beyond the Horizon*; 1966.

12. Tennyson and Millet; *Idylls of the King* and *The King's Henchman*; 1965.

NORTON, W. W. & CO., INC.
55 5th AVE., NEW YORK, N.Y. 10003

1. Edman, Irwin; *Arts and the Man*; 154 p.; $1.85; Adv. H.S., Coll. Brief discussion of "the experience of the arts and the implications of art in civilization."

2. Grout, Donald Jay; *A History of Western Music*; 515 p.; 1964; H.S., Coll. Designed for the shorter course in the history of

music; a chronological treatment covering the changes in musical style and development of instruments, notation, music-printing and biographies of composers. 113 musical illustrations, glossary, bibliography and chronology.

3. Morey, C. R.; *Christian Art*; 120 p.; 1935; $1.25; H.S., Coll. Medieval and Renaissance art and architecture as cultural and philosophical expression. 50 illustrative plates.

OXFORD UNIVERSITY PRESS, INC.
417 FIFTH AVE., NEW YORK, N.Y. 10016

1. Ellman, Richard and Feidelson, Jr., eds.; *The Modern Tradition*; 948 p.; 1965; H.S., Coll. An exploration of the modern tradition in literature in the form of an anthology of statements by writers, artists, scientists, and philosophers arranged by themes: symbolism, realism, nature, cultural history, the unconscious, myth, existence, and faith.
2. Kane, Thomas S. and Peters, eds.; *Writing Prose: Techniques and Purposes*; 486 p.; 1964; H.S., Coll. A text which attempts to teach writing through the presentation of models which show the diversity of subjects, purposes, and techniques in good prose. Grouped by type.
3. Lawler, James R.; *An Anthology of French Poetry*; 144 p.; 1961; H.S., Coll. An introductory survey of French poetry since the Renaissance. Guide to degree of linguistic difficulty, vocabularly list.
4. Litz, A. Walton, ed.; *Modern American Fiction: Essays in Criticism*; 365 p.; 1963; $2.25; H.S., Coll. Commentaries on the major writers of American fiction, from Stephen Crane to the present. Examinations of range of work as well as decisive models. Emphasis on Fitzgerald, Faulkner, Hemingway.
5. Rosenthal, M. L.; *The Modern Poets*; 288 p.; 1965; $2.25; H.S., Coll. Survey of poets from Yeats, Pound and Eliot to Lawrence, Crane, Thomas, and their successors.

PENGUIN BOOKS, INC.
330 CLIPPED MILL RD., BALTIMORE, MD. 21211

THE PENGUIN ENGLISH LIBRARY

A series in paperback, perfect binding, of classics intended to survey such works in English since the fifteenth century. Authoritative introductions ,notes; $.95–$1.95; H.S., Coll.
1. Austen, Jane; *Emma*; 1966.
2. Austen, Jane; *Mansfield Park*; 1966.
3. Austen, Jane; *Persuasion*; 1965.
4. Bronte, Charlotte; *Jane Eyre*; 1966.
5. Bronte, Emily; *Wuthering Heights*; 1965.
6. Bunyan, John; *The Pilgrim's Progress*; 1965.

177

7. Butler, Samuel; *The Way of All Flesh*; 1966.
8. Collins, Wilkie; *The Moonstone*; 1966.
9. DeFoe, Daniel; *A Journal of the Plague Year*; 1966.
10. DeFoe, Daniel; *Robinson Crusoe*; 1965.
11. Dickens, Charles; *David Copperfield*; 1966.
12. Dickens, Charles; *Great Expectations*; 1965.
13. Dickens, Charles; *Oliver Twist*; 1966.
14. Eliot, George; *Middlemarch*; 1965.
15. Fielding, Henry; *Tom Jones*; 1966.
16. Johnson, Ben; *Three Comedies*; 1966.
17. Tourneur, Webster, and Middleton; *Three Jacobean Tragedies;* 1965.
18. Twain, Mark; *The Adventures of Huckleberry Finn*; 1966.

ADDITIONAL TITLES
1. Cicero; *Selected Works*; 271 p.; 1965; $.95; H.S., Coll. Contents include *Against Verres I*, 23 letters, *Second Philippic Against Antony*, *On Duty III*, *On Old Age*. List of surviving works, genealogical tables, glossary, maps.
2. Hall, Donald, ed.; *Contemporary American Poetry*; 200 p.; 1962; $1.25; H.S., Coll. A paper edition which shows the work of 25 poets born after 1914. Several examples of the work of each are included. Introduction.
3. Pevsner, Nikolaus; *An Outline of European Architecture*; 496 p.; 1963; $2.25; H.S., Coll. A chronological history from the 4th century to the present; as cultural artifacts and omitting fringe geographic areas. Bibliog. 295 illustrations.
4. Richards, J. M.; *An Introduction to Modern Architecture*; 184 p.; 1962; $2.25; H.S., Coll. An explanation of the "New architecture" for the layman; 48 pages of illustrations; sketches and diagrams; bibliography.

PHAIDON PRESS LTD.
5 CROMWELL PLACE, LONDON SW 7, ENGLAND

1. Gombrich, E.H.; *The Story of Art*; 484 p.; 1966; distributed by Oxford U. Press; H.S., Coll. An introduction to art history for both young people and adults. 384 illustrations match text discussion which is clear and interesting. Chronological. Paper covered.
2. Rosenberg, Jakob; *Rembrandt: Life and Work*; 342 p.; 1964; $8.50; distributed by the N. Y. Graphic Society.; H.S., Coll. A standard work in one volume, unabridged and revised. Covers Rembrandt's life and portraits, landscapes, biblical scenes and genre painting in separate chapters. Extensive notes and comment on the artist in his time.
3. Sherer, Margaret R.; *The Legends of Troy in Art and Literature;*

304 p.; 1964; $7.95; distributed by the Met. Museum of Art; H.S., Coll. Legends of the *Illiad, Odyssey, Aeneid,* and variations are discussed and illustrated with 190 plates ranging from Greek vase paintings to modern American interpretations. Two extensive appendices list works of art, literature and music dealing with Trojan themes.

PITMAN PUBLISHING CORP.
20 E. 46th ST., NEW YORK, N.Y. 10017

1. Myron, Robert; *Prehistoric Art;* 1964; $1.00; H.S., Coll. A highly illustrated introductory discussion of prehistoric painting and sculpture with a section on modern similarity.
2. Read, Herbert; *Art Now;* 131 p. text, 196 plates; 1960; H.S., Coll. A new revision of the famous "introduction to the theory of modern painting and sculpture." A chronological approach from Reynolds to Klee.
3. Sternberg, Harry; *Realistic/Abstract Art;* 1959; $1.00; H.S. Visual demonstration and practical working procedures for an introduction to an understanding of contemporary art. The range from illusionistic realism to complete abstraction is shown in a variety of themes.

PLATT & MUNK, INC.
200 FIFTH AVE., NEW YORK, N.Y. 10010

GREAT WRITERS COLLECTION; Upper Elem., H.S.; $3.97 ea.; cloth volumes containing several of the best works —complete or excerpts—of writers especially popular with young people. A biographical note for each author.

1. Doyle, Sir Arthur Conan; *Conan Doyle Stories;* 1960.
2. Harte, Bret; *Stories of the Early West;* 1964; contains 17 stories.
3. Kipling, Rudyard; *Kipling Stories: 28 Tales;* 1960.
4. London, Jack; *Jack London Stories;* 1960; contains 20 stories.
5. Melville, Herman; *Moby Dick; Typee; Billy Budd;* 1964.
6. Henry, O.; *O. Henry Short Stories;* 1962; contains 35 stories.
7. Poe, Edgar Allan; *Edgar Allan Poe Stories;* 1961; contains 27 stories.
8. Stevenson, Robert Louis; *Great Tales of Mystery and Adventure;* 1965; contains 11 stories.
9. Twain, Mark; *The Adventures of Tom Sawyer; The Adventures of Huckleberry Finn;* 1960.
10. Verne, Jules; *20,000 Leagues Under the Sea; Around the Moon;* 1965.
11. Wells, H. G.; *The War of the Worlds; The Time Machine; Selected Short Stories;* 1963.

ADDITIONAL TITLES
1. Chase, Alice Elizabeth; *Famous Artists of the Past;* 120 p.; 1964; $6.39; H.S. The lives and works of 27 artists in text and 177

reproductions (44 color). Treatments are short but extensively illustrated and in flowing text.

POCKET BOOKS, INC.
630 FIFTH AVE., NEW YORK, N.Y. 10020

1. Mitchell, Margaret; *Gone With the Wind*; 862 p.; 1964; $1.25; H.S., Coll. The classic story of the disintegration of the antebellum South. Paperback.

PRAEGER, FREDERICK A., INC.
111 FOURTH AVE., NEW YORK, N.Y. 10003

1. Goodrich, Lloyd, and Baur; *American Art of Our Century*; 305 p.; 1961; $15.00; H.S., Coll. American art and artists of the 20th century; trends in sculpture, drawing and painting, 81 color plates, 166 black and white illustrations from the Whitney Museum collection. Treatment is chronological and by movements or schools.

PRATT, J. LOWELL & CO.
15 E. 48th ST., NEW YORK, N.Y. 10017

1. Wakefield, Eleanor Ely; *Folk Dancing in America*; 221 p.; 1966; $3.95; H.S., Coll., T. Contains an historical survey, educational value and methods of teaching as well as dances from many nations linked to the history of the U.S. List of recordings, classification, bibliography.

PUTNAM'S, G. P., SONS
200 MADISON AVE., NEW YORK, N.Y. 10016

1. Diez, Ernst; *The Ancient Worlds of Asia: From Mesopotamia to the Yellow River*; 240 p.; 1961; $4.50; H.S. Survey of Asian cultures from the time of Noah to 19th century Mandalay— 5,000 years. Both written and archaeological sources to portray daily life. Maps, photos.
2. Hamlin, Talbot; *Architecture Through the Ages*; 684 p.; 1953; $9.50; H.S., Coll. "The story of building in relation to man's progress." Materials and form as answers to needs. Chronological treatment. Extensive illustrations and sketches.
3. Peyser, Ethel, and Baur; *How Opera Grew*; 495 p.; $6.00; H.S. The history of opera from 7th century B.C. Greece to Stravinsky and Menotti. The techniques of the art form including the orchestra, ballets, scenery, etc. are discussed.
4. Slavita, Chana; *Let's Go to a Ballet*; 45 p.; 1959; Elem. An illustrated introduction to the art form and the mechanics behind the ballet performance. Correlated activities, glossary.

RANDOM HOUSE INC.
457 MADISON AVE., NEW YORK, N.Y. 10002

1. Clark, Eleanor; *The Song of Roland*; 53 p.; 1960; $1.50; Elem. A retelling of Roland's stand at Roncevaux with two-color illustrations.

180

2. Kramer, Nora, ed.; *The Grandma Moses Storybook*; 141 p.; 1961; $5.95; Elem., H.S. Illustrated with paintings by Grandma Moses; stories and poems for young people by James Russell Lowell, Robert Frost, Rachel Field and others.
3. Ottenberg, Simon and Phoebe, eds.; *Cultures and Societies of Africa*; 564 p.; 1960; H.S., Coll. A "Systematic collection of some of the most important anthropological writings on Africa." Initial section on geography, language, culture contact, religion, folklore, etc. is followed by sections on people and environment, social groupings, authority and government, values, religion and aesthetics and culture contact. Extensive bibliography.

REILLY & LEE CO.
114 W. ILLINOIS ST., CHICAGO, ILLINOIS 60610

1. Bogan, Louise, and Smith, eds.; *The Golden Journey: Poems for Young People*; 275 p.; 1965; $5.95; Elem., H.S. A beautifully presented anthology of a variety of poems from many pens and times which gives the fullest possible insight into the art form for the young reader. 107 authors, over 200 poems.

REINHOLD PUBLISHING CORP.
430 PARK AVE., NEW YORK, N.Y. 10022

ART HORIZONS SERIES; 1964; $5.50; H.S., Coll. A series of art instruction books by artists—teachers which present techniques and projects as well as extensive illustrations of both.
1. Ford, Betty Davenport; *Ceramic Sculpture*; 100 p.
2. Krevitsky, Nik; *Batik: Art and Craft*; 68 p.

ADDITIONAL TITLES
1. Crosby, Theo; *Architecture: City Sense*; 95 p.; 1965; $2.25; H.S., Coll. An environmental approach to the need for regeneration of existing urban areas. Examples largely English but with universality.
2. Gore, Frederick; *Painting: Some Basic Principles*; 95 p.; 1965; $2.25; H.S., Coll. Consideration of the drawings, color, composition and artistic rationale of painting by an eminent artist. Numerous illustrations.
3. Myers, Bernard; *Sculpture: Form and Method*; 95 p.; 1965; $2.25; H.S., Coll. Historic survey of sculpture with explanation of methods and materials as well as place in its culture. Illustrated.

ST. MARTIN'S PRESS, INC.
175 5th AVE., NEW YORK, N.Y. 10010

1. Bowra, C. M.; *Heroic Poetry*; 587 p.; 1964; H.S., Coll. An authoritative study of the heroic, narrative poem through comparison of texts from 30 countries in terms of content and technique.

2. Lynch, Patrick; *Man Makes His World*; 64 p.; 1959; Elem. A history of the world with emphasis on man's achievements—institutions, inventions, discoveries, customs.

SCARECROW PRESS INC.
257 PARK AVE. S., NEW YORK, N.Y. 10010

1. Clapp, Jane; *Art in "Life"*; 504 p.; 1959; $12.50; Ref., 5 up. An index of art reproductions contained in "Life" magazine from its beginning in 1936 through 1956. Also lists selected photographs of architecture, the decorative arts, historic and literary personages and of artists. Black and white indicated.
2. Clapp, Jane; *Art in "Life"—Supplement 1965*; 379 p.; 1965; $8.50; Ref., 5 up. Supplement I from 1957–1963. Lists selected photos of events, objects, persons in sciences and theater and of topical interest. Black and white indicated.

SCOTT, FORESMAN & CO.
1900 E. LAKE AVE., GLENWOOD, ILL. 60025

AMERICA READS SERIES; Pooley, gen. ed.; Textbook anthologies arranged by literary form within each volume. Composition guide, glossaries. Explication and review contains test tables and tests on vocabulary and content. Student and teacher editions. Teacher's Resource Book presents reprints of commentary, study aids, and teaching guides.

1. *Outlooks Through Literature*; 752 p.; 1964; $3.87; grade 9.
2. *Exploring Life Through Literature*; 754 p.; 1964; $3.93; grade 10; two editions: 1) with *Silas Marner* 2) with *The Pearl, Master and Man,* and *Secret Sharer.*
3. *The U.S. in Literature*; 813 p.; $4.14; 1963; grade 11.
4. *England in Literature*; 813 p.; 1963; $4.20; grade 12.

ADDITIONAL TITLES
1. Arbuthnot, May Hill; *The Arbuthnot Anthology of Children's Literature*; 443 p.; 1961; grades 4–8, T. The well-known anthology of poetry, choral selections, folk and fairy tales, fables, myths and epics, fiction and biography. An extensive bibliography.

SCRIBNER'S, CHARLES SONS
597 FIFTH AVE., NEW YORK, N.Y. 10017

SCRIBNER RESEARCH ANTHOLOGY SERIES; A series of paper volumes which are collections of written sources on a single problem designed to be used in the preparation of a research paper. Each contains an introduction to the topic, a guide, and suggested topics for research. H.S., Coll.

1. Baker, Carlos; *Ernest Hemingway*; 200 p.; 1962; Critiques of "The Sun also Rises", "A Farewell to Arms", "For Whom the Bell Tolls", and "The Old Man and the Sea".

2. Cowley and Cowley; *Fitzgerald and the Jazz Age*; 192 p.; 1966.
3. Holman, C. Hugh; *The World of Thomas Wolfe*; 1962; 185 p.
4. Hurrell, John D.; *Two Modern American Tragedies*; 152 p.; 1961; Reviews and criticism of "Death of a Salesman" and "A Streetcar Named Desire".
5. McCann, Richard Dyer; *Film and Society*; 180 p.; 1964.
6. Markels, Julian; *Shakespeare's "Julius Caesar"*; 120 p.; 1961.
7. Stafford, Wm. T.; *James' "Daisy Miller"*; 166 p.; 1963; The story, the play, the critics.
8. Weintraub, Stanley; *C. P. Snow: A Spectrum*; 155 p.; 1963; science, criticism, fiction.

ADDITIONAL TITLES

1. Brown, Marcia; *The Flying Carpet*; 1956; $2.65; Elem. A retelling from the Burton translation of one of the "lesser" Arabian nights. Illustrated by the adapter.
2. Brown, Marcia; *Once a Mouse—A Fable Cut in Wood*; 1961; $3.12; Elem. A fable of ancient India retold from the *Hitopadesa* and given full-page illustrations. A Caldecott book.
3. Clark, J. Kent, and Piper, eds.; *Dimensions in Drama: Six Plays of Crime and Punishment*; 573 p.; 1964; H.S., Coll. Six plays selected for variety as well as continuity—variety in origin, similarity in theme. *Oedipus Rex, The Beggar's Opera, Rosmersholm, All My Sons, MacBeth,* and *No Exit*. Discussion questions.
4. Davenport, Wm. H., and Siegal, eds.; *Biography: Past and Present —Selections and Critical Essays*; 472 p.; 1965; H.S., Coll. Classical and modern biography with critical and historical essays. Variety, readability, representativeness rather than the most usual selections. Authoritative texts, some modernized. Suggestions for reading and writing. PBK.
5. Grimm Bros.; *The Shoemaker and the Elves*; 1960; Elem. A translation of one of the most famous of the Grimms' "Hausmarchen" with original illusrations.
6. Konopnicka, Maria; *The Golden Seed*; 1962; Elem. Adaptation of a well-known Polish story or literary folktale with original illustration. Picture of life in Medieval Poland.
7. Stefanson, Evelyn; *Here Is Alaska*; 171 p.; 1959; H.S. An authoritative description of Alaska which contains much ethnological material on the Indian and Eskimo. Extensively illustrated.
8. Uchida, Yoshiko; *The Sea of Gold and Other Tales from Japan*; 135 p.; 1965; Elem. Adaptations of 12 traditional Japanese folk tales, illustrated with charcoal. Glossary, elementary type.

SEABURY PRESS, INC.
815 SECOND AVE., NEW YORK, N.Y. 10017

1. Abbott, Anthony S.; *Shaw and Christianity*; 221 p.; 1965; $4.95; 12–Coll. Shaw as "a serious critic" of Christianity. Six plays are examined in terms of religious themes: *Devil's Disciple, Shewing-up of Blanco Posnet, Major Babara, Androcles and the Lion, Simpleton of the Unexpected Isles.* Chapters on Shaw's background, artistic growth and final importance for the Christian.

SILVER BURDETT CO.
PARK AVE. AND COLUMBIA RD., MORRISTOWN, N.J. 07960

1. Cooper, and others; *Music in Our Life*; 225 p. 1967; $3.76; Jr. H.S. Traditional and professional music which emphasizes the role music plays in the total culture. Background information confined to teacher's ed. Suggestions for parallel listening.

2. Cooper, and others; *Music in Our Times*; 229 p.; 1967; $3.84; Jr. H.S. Selections from Contemporary American life as well as its background and ethnic variety.

3. Sabin, Frances E.; *Classical Myths That Live Today*; 347 p.; 1958; Elem., Jr. H.S. A collection of the best known Greek and Roman myths in simple language. Sections on the place of these myths today. Illustrated.

4. Serposs, Emile H., and Singleton; *Music in Our Heritage*; 230 p.; 1963; $4.00; H.S. Vocal and instrumental selections which "represent a stylistic sampling of music, literature of the past six centuries." Traditional and symphonic music. Source book provides background material and relates selections to famous paintings.

SIMON AND SCHUSTER, INC.
630 FIFTH AVE., NEW YORK, N.Y. 10020

1. Canaday, John; *Mainstreams of Modern Art*; 553 p.; 1959; $15.00; H.S., Coll. An authoritative guide to modern art including historical background, more than 700 illustrations and non-technical text.

2. Emmerich, Andre; *Art Before Columbus*; 249 p.; 1963; $10.00; H.S., Coll. The Olmecs, Toltecs, Mixtecs, Huaxtecs, Zapotecs, Mayas and Aztecs—their art as related to the total culture. Illustrated with over 150 photos of murals, sculpture, architecture, jewelry, etc.

3. Laver, James; *Costume Through the Ages*; 144 p.; 1963; $4.95; All. A continuous series of drawings depicting costume from the first century A.D. to 1930. Relative space reveals the rate of change in fashion and notes cite the sources for each item.

SOUTHERN ILLINOIS UNIVERSITY PRESS
CARBONDALE, ILL. 62901
1. Weiss, Paul; *The World of Art*; 193 p.; 1964; $4.50 Coll. A philo-
sophical examination of art influenced by Susanne Langer
and which inquires into the issues central to all the creative
arts.

SUMMY-BIRCHARD PUBLISHING CO.
1834 RIDGE AVE., EVANSTON, ILL. 60204
1. Best, Florence C.; *Music in the Making*; 96 p.; 1960; $2.80; Elem.,
Jr. H.S. A workbook with exercises on appreciation, the technique and form of music.

TIME-LIFE BOOKS DIVISION OF TIME, INC.
TIME & LIFE BLDG., NEW YORK, N.Y. 10020
1. Bowra, C. M., and Time-Life eds.; *Classical Greece*; 186 p.; 1965;
$3.95; H.S. One of a series of books which portray civilizations
through text by a leading authority and extensive illustration.
Emphasis is on an outline of the culture using the arts of the
culture for portrayal.
2. Coughlan, Robert, and Time-Life eds.; *The World of Michelangelo, 1475–1564*; 202 p.; 1966; $4.95; H.S. One of a series of
books on art history as studied through masters of medieval
and modern times. Extensive illustration.

TUTTLE, CHARLES E. CO.
28 S. MAIN ST., RUTLAND, VT. 05701
CUSTOMS AND CULTURE SERIES; $3.95; Elem.–Coll.
Material on the geography, history, education, celebrations,
beliefs, arts, language and stories of the geographic area.
1. Crawford, Ann Caddell; *Customs and Culture of Vietnam*; 259 p.;
1966.
2. Zabilka, Gladys; *Customs and Culture of Okinawa*; 200 p.; 1959.
3. Zabilka, Gladys; *Customs and Culture of the Philippines*; 195 p.;
1963.

ADDITIONAL TITLES

1. Dorson, Richard M.; *Folk Legends of Japan*; 256 p.; 1962; $4.75;
Elem.–Coll. Transcriptions of over 100 oral legends from a
country rich in them. Introduction to the significance of the
legend. Illustrated, legend sources, bibliography.
2. Hillier, J.; *The Japanese Print: A New Approach*; 184 p.; 1960;
$5.25; H.S., Coll. Some less known masters of the print ap-
proached through his particular contribution to the total art
form. 64 Illus.
3. Kelly, Jr., John M.; *Folk Songs Hawaii Sings*; 80 p.; 1962; $4.95;
Elem., Sec. Twenty-seven songs arranged for piano and voice
with background notes. Arranged by country of origin—

Hawaii, Samoa, Uvea, Japan, Philippines, China, and Korea. Native and English lyrics.

4. Lytle, Ruby; *What Is the Moon? . . . Japanese Haiku Sequence*; 32 p.; 1965; $1.00; Elem., H.S. Explanation of Haiku form and illustrated answers to the title question as asked by a Siamese kitten.

5. Morris, Ivan, ed.; *Modern Japanese Stories: An Anthology*; 512 p.; 1962; $6.50; H.S. Twenty-five short stories of Japan after 1910. Introduction of 22 pages surveys the field. Authoritative translations. Bibliography.

6. Munsterberg, Hugo; *The Arts of Japan: An Illustrated History*; 201 p.; 1962; $2.95; H.S. Painting, sculpture, architecture and handicrafts treated by period and art form. 121 illustrative plates, 12 in color. The various influences are discussed as well as prehistoric art. Available in cloth ed.

7. Sakade, Florence, ed.; *Japanese Children's Favorite Stories*; 120 p.; 1958; $3.50; Elem. Twenty traditional stories with original illustrations.

8. So-Un, Kim; *The Story Bag: A Collection of Korean Folktales*; 229 p.; 1955; $1.50; Elem.–Coll. Thirty traditional stories collected by the author, some versions of world-wide tales.

9. Toda, Kenji; *Japanese Painting: A Brief History*; 102 p.; 1965; $2.50; H.S. A paperback survey of 1,000 years of Japanese painting by an outstanding authority. Division into the Chinese, Buddhist and Japanese schools, full page, black and white illustrations.

UNIVERSITY OF CHICAGO PRESS
5750 ELLIS AVENUE, CHICAGO, ILLINOIS 60637

1. Dorson, Richard M.; *American Folklore*; 328 p.; 1959; $.95 paper; Secondary, college, teachers. The broad field of folklore by an American authority. The authentic is separated from the synthetic; the folk hero, Colonial lore, the Negro, immigrant and modern American are treated in interesting text. Motifs and tale types are noted.

2. Taylor, Joshua C.; *Learning to Look*; 152 p.; 1957; $1.95; paper ed.; H.S., Coll. The standard work on analysis and comprehension of the visual arts, intended for humanities courses as guide and reference.

UNIVERSITY OF ILLINOIS PRESS
URBANA, ILL. 61801

1. Steward, Julian H.; *Theory of Culture Change*; 222 p.; 1955–1963; Coll., T. Concepts and methods for making comparative cultural studies. Application is made to seven cultures from the Shoshone Indians to contemporary Puerto Rico.

UNIVERSITY OF TORONTO PRESS
FRONT CAMPUS , TORONTO 5, ONTARIO, CANADA

1. Carpenter, E. and others; *Eskimo;* 1959; $3.95; H.S., Coll. Sketches by Frederick Varley, the Robert Flaherty collection of Eskimo carvings and text by anthropologist Edmund Carpenter combine to portray Eskimo art and culture. Emphasis of the text is on Eskimo spatial orientation—acoustic rather than visual thesis.

UNIVERSITY OF WISCONSIN PRESS
BOX 1379, MADISON, WISCONSIN 53701

1. Stewart, Janice S.; *The Folk Arts of Norway;* 228 p.; 1953; $10.00; H.S., Coll. Analysis of the "peasant arts" of Norway and their function. Includes rosemailing, metal working, furniture, architecture, textiles, regional costumes, and is illustrated with over 200 color and black and white plates.

VAN NOSTRAND, D., CO. INC.
120 ALEXANDER ST., PRINCETON, N.J. 08540

1. Sabine, Ellen S.; *American Folk Art;* 129 p.; 1958; $8.95; Elem., H.S., Primarily a book of instruction on the reproduction of "Country painting" on tin, wood, and glass as well as fraktur of the Penn. German. Designs shown in scale.

VIKING PRESS, INC.
625 MADISON AVE., NEW YORK, N.Y. 10022

COMPASS HISTORY OF ART SERIES; $2.25; H.S., Coll. Paperback, perfect binding, text by world experts (30–50 pages). 176 color and black and white full page illustrations, fold-out listing.

1. Ainaud, Juan; *Romanesque Painting;* 1963.
2. Carli, Gudiol, and Souchal; *Gothic Painting;* 1965.
3. Chatzidakis, Manolis, and Grabar; *Byzantine and Early Medieval Painting;* 1965.
4. Cogniat, Raymond; *17th Century Painting;* 1964.
5. Devambez; *Greek Painting;* 1962.
6. DuBourguet, S. J., Pierre; *Early Christian Painting;* 1965.
7. Jaffe, H. L. C.; *Twentieth Century Painting;* 1963.
8. Mitchell, Sabrina; *Medieval Manuscript Painting;* 1964.
9. Peilley, Georges; *Nineteenth Century Painting;* 1964.
10. Photiades, Wassily; *Eighteenth Century Painting;* 1963.
11. Russoli, Franco; *Renaissance Painting;* 1962.
12. Steinico, Arturo; *Roman and Etruscan Painting;* 1963.

VIKING PORTABLES SERIES

1. Auden, W. H.; *The Portable Greek Reader;* 726 p.; 1948; $1.85; H.S., Coll. A comprehensive anthology of Greek literature in leading translations with arrangment by topics such as the

hero, nature, man, society, cosmogonies and cosmologies. Chronological outline of classical Greek civilizations.

2. Brinton, Crane, ed.; *The Portable Age of Reason Reader*; 628 p.; 1956; $1.85; H.S., Coll. Manners, morals and politics; philosophy and natural science, religion, literature, memoirs and letters.

3. Davenport, Basil; *The Portable Roman Reader*; 672 p.; 1951; $1.85; H.S., Coll. "The culture of the Roman state" in leading translations from Cicero to Augustine.

4. Hugo, Howard E., ed.; *The Portable Romantic Reader*; 640 p.; 1957; $1.85; H.S., Coll. 1756–1848. Self-image, the man of feeling, hero and fatal woman, the past, nature, revolutions, the artist.

5. Ross, J. B., McLaughlin, eds.; *The Portable Medieval Reader*; 687 p.; 1949; $1.85; H.S., Coll. Writings from 1050–1500. *The Body Social, The Christian Commonwealth, the House of Fame, The World Picture, The Noble Castle*. Chronology.

6. Ross, J. B., McLaughlin, eds.; *The Portable Renaissance Reader*; 756 p.; 1963; $1.85; H.S., Coll. Italy and N. Europe, 1400–1600. *An Age of Gold, The City of Man, The Study of Man, The Book of Nature, The Kingdom of God*. Chronology, bibliography.

ADDITIONAL TITLES

1. Asbjornsen and Moe; *Norwegian Folk Tales*; 189 p.; $4.53; grade 5 up. Thirty-five tales from the collection of Peter Christian Asbjornsen and Jorgen Moe translated and illustrated by specialists in Scandinavian lore and literature. Original illustrations of the 1881 edition. A classic collection.

2. Bailey, Carolyn S.; *Pioneer Art in America*; 220 p.; 1944; $4.13; Grades 5–8. Stories of various American "folk artists and their art forms—iron, glass, silver, wall painting, etc." With a final section on Grant Wood. Puts arts and crafts into their historic perspective.

3. Cali, Francois; *The Spanish Arts of Latin America*; 181 p.; 1961; $12.50; H.S., Coll., Elem. T. An extensively illustrated (181 photogravure plates, 4 color plates) examination of the architecture, painting, sculpture of the Spanish period including the Indian influence on the art of New Spain.

4. Campbell, Joseph; *The Masks of God: Oriental Mythology*; 516 p.; 1962; $7.50; H.S., Coll. An analysis of non-Western mythology, its relation to religions in light of archaeology, anthropology and psychology.

5. Cheney, Sheldon; *The Story of Modern Art*; 708 p.; 1958; H.S.,

Coll., T. Modern art from 1800 examined and explained in a chronological manner, extensively illustrated.

6. Donat, John, ed.; *World Architecture II*; 217 p.; 1965; $15.00; H.S., Coll. Contributions from 17 countries profusely illustrated, attempt to explain to the layman what architects are thinking and doing today.

7. Dorra, Henri; *The American Muse*; 161 p.; 1961; $10.00; H.S., T. The linking of painting, poetry and prose to tell the story of American creative genius. Text explains the six major trends such as the cults of nature and experience, the haunted mind, social protest, etc.

8. Ferres, John H., ed.; *Sherwood Anderson: Winesburg, Ohio—Text and Criticism*; 511 p.; 1966; $1.95; H.S., Coll. A critical edition of a significant work which includes author statements, memoirs, letters, early reviews and critical essays. Annotated bibliog., topics for the student, etc.

9. Friedman, Albert B., ed.; *The Viking Book of Folk Ballads of the English-Speaking World*; 469 p.; 1956; $2.25; All. Arranged by theme with notes on background and version. Introduction, bibliog. and glossary. Variants included for many ballads.

10. Holme, Bryan; *Drawings to Live With*; 156 p.; 1966; $4.13; Upper Elem., H.S. Sketches: pen, pencil, chalk; prints; illustrations; humorous drawings from the world in all ages. Appreciation and understanding—subject and technique.

11. Holme, Bryan; *Pictures to Live With*; 149 p.; 1959; $4.50; Upper Elem., H.S. Includes American paintings, drawings, sculpture, lithographs, of every description and period with commentary, explanation and citation for each. Section on European heritage.

12. McCloskey, Robert; *Time of Wonder*; 63 p.; 1958; $3.37; Elem. A Caldecott book which tells of a Maine island in summer in rhythmic prose and outstanding watercolor illustrations.

13. Robinson, Ethel Fay, and Thomas P.; *Houses in America*; 231 p.; 1936; $4.13; Upper Elem., H.S. The American tradition in colonial architecture—houses examined in terms of their builders, European antecedents and native environment. Illustrated with 180 pencil drawings.

14. Shippen, Katherine B. and Seidlova; *The Heritage of Music*; 285 p.; 1963; $5.63; H.S. Western music from its beginnings chronologically, to today with concentration on professional musicians.

15. Steinbeck, John; *The Pearl; The Red Pony*; 181 p.; 1965; $1.25; Elem., H.S. Complete texts of both works with illustrations in a perfect binding.

16. Stern, Milton R. and Gross, eds.; *American Literary Survey*, four volumes; 520–560 p. ea.; 1962; H.S. Vol. I: Colonial and Federal to 1800; II: American Romantics 1800–1860; III: Nation and Region 1860–1900; IV: The Twentieth Century. An anthology of the variety and best of American literature; many less common selections.

VINTAGE BOOKS/RANDOM HOUSE INC.
457 MADISON AVE., NEW YORK, N.Y. 10022

1. Hauser, Arnold; *The Social History of Art*, four volumes; 225–250 p. ea.; 1951; $1.45 ea.; H.S., Coll. Vol. I—prehistoric, ancient, oriental, Greece and Rome, Middle Ages; II—Renaissance, Mannerism, Baroque; III—Rococo, Classicism, Romanticism; IV—Naturalism, Impressionism, The Film Age. Each paper volume treats literature, the visual arts, and drama in the context of social history. Center section of 24 reproductions.

WALKER & CO.
720 FIFTH AVE., NEW YORK, N.Y. 10019

1. Baines, Anthony, ed.; *Musical Instruments Thru the Ages*; 314 p.; $10.00; H.S., Coll., T. The Evolution of musical instruments in many cultures and the interrelationship with music itself. Sixteen Musicologists of the Galpin Society discuss the instruments by groups. Glossary, bibliography, many illustrations.

WASHINGTON SQ. PRESS INC,
DIV. OF SIMON AND SCHUSTER, INC.
630 FIFTH AVE., NEW YORK, N.Y. 10020

ANTA SERIES OF DISTINGUISHED PLAYS; $.60; H.S., Coll.

1. Freedley, George, ed.; *Three Plays by Maxwell Anderson*; 292 p.; 1962; contains *Joan of Lorraine, Valley Forge, Journey to Jerusalem*.
2. Mersand, Joseph, ed.; *Three Plays About Doctors*; 294 p.; 1961; contains Ibsen's *An Enemy of the People*, Kingsley's *Man in White*, and Howard's *Yellow Jack*.
3. Mersand, Joseph, ed.; *Three Plays About Marriage*; 298 p.; 1962; contains Kelly's *Craig's Wife*, Howard's *They Know What They Wanted*, and Barry's *Holiday*.
4. Mersand, Joseph, ed.; *Three Dramas of American Individualism*; 265 p.; 1961; *Golden Boy, High Tor*, and *The Magnificent Yankee*.
5. Mersand, Joseph, ed.; *Three Dramas of American Realism*; 312 p.; 1961; contains Sherwood's *Idiots' Delight*, Rice's *Street Scene*, and Saroyan's *The Time of Your Life*.
6. Yurka, Blanche, ed.; *Three Scandinavian Plays*; 266 p.; 1962; Strindberg's *The Father*, Ibsen's *The Lady from the Sea*, and *The Wild Duck*.

READER'S ENRICHMENT SERIES; H.S.; Paper cover, perfect binding, unabridged, series of classics with supplement covering aids to study, background materials, etc. Teacher's editions $2.00 and $2.50; regular $.60 and $.75.
1. Day, Clarence; *Life With Mother*; 1965.
2. Defoe, Daniel; *Robinson Crusoe*; 1963.
3. DuMaurier, Daphne; *Rebecca*; 1965.
4. Eliot, George; *Silas Marner*; 1964.
5. Hardy, Thomas; *The Mayor of Casterbridge*; 1964.
6. Hardy, Thomas; *The Return of the Native*; 1964.
7. Hawthorne, Nathaniel; *The Scarlet Letter*; 1963.
8. Landon, Margaret; *Anna and the King of Siam* (abridged); 1963.
9. London, Jack; *The Call of the Wild*; 1963.
10. Shakespeare, William; *Hamlet*; 1966.
11. Stevenson, Robert Louis; *Treasure Island*; 1963.
12. Twain, Mark; *The Adventures of Tom Sawyer*; 1963.

ADDITIONAL TITLES
1. D'Espezel, Pierre and Fosca; *A Concise Illustrated History of European Painting*; 333 p.; 1961; $.90; H.S., Coll. Abridged edition of "The Pageant of Painting". 64 pages of reproductions, half in color.
2. Flexner, James Thomas; *The Pocket History of American Painting*; 18 p.; 1950; $.60; H.S., 52 illustrations from all of the major American painters; authoritative text.
3. Hansen, Harry, ed.; *The Pocket Book of O. Henry Stories*; 238 p.; 1948; $.45; H.S., Coll. 30 stories.
4. Janson and Janson; *The Picture History of Painting*; 224 p.; 1961; $1.45; H.S., Coll. Abridged edition. 100 black and white, 33 color illustrations from cave painting to Dali.
5. DeOnis, Harriet, ed.; *Spanish Stories and Tales*; 228 p.; 1962; $.45; 23 short stories.

WATERLOO MUSIC CO. LIMITED
WATERLOO, ONTARIO, CANADA
1. Bissell, K.; *Festival Songs for S.A.B.*; 23 p.; 1961; H.S. Eleven folk and traditional songs and hymns of English, Canadian, and American origin.
2. Fowke and Johnston; *Folk Songs of Canada*; 91 p.; 1954; Upper Elem., H.S. Songs and ballads arranged for S.A.T.B. unisons with some for two-part, S.A.B., T.T.B.B., and T.B.B. French and English lyrics. Most are traditional; some modern. Grade level suggested, arranged by theme.
3. Fowke and Johnston; *Folk Songs of Quebec*; 89 p.; 1958; H.S. 44 songs and ballads with English and French words arranged by theme. Chord notation and explanation of version pre-

sented with an article on singing in French.

4. Johnston, Richard; *Chansons Canadiennes-Francaises*; 59 p.; 1964; Upper Elem., H.S. French-Canadian folk songs arranged for two voices.

WAYNE STATE UNIVERSITY PRESS
5980 CASS AVE., DETROIT, MICH. 48202

1. Pawlowska, Harriet M., ed.; *Merrily We Sing: 105 Polish Folksongs*; 263 p.; 1961; All. Songs collected and transcribed from 10 informants in the Polish community of Detroit. Both Polish and English words to carols, ballads, songs. Notes, bibliog., analysis of "Child 4" in 15 versions.

WRITER'S DIGEST
22 E. 12th ST., CINCINNATI, OHIO 45201

1. Jerome, Judson; *The Poet and the Poem*; 226 p.; 1963; $4.50; H.S., Coll. Discussion of what is involved in the writing of "good" poetry by a poet and editor. Divided into two parts, the first deals with the sensibilities and attitudes of the poet, the second and larger, with technique.

YALE UNIVERSITY PRESS
92A YALE STATION, NEW HAVEN, CONN. 06520

1. Cassirer, Ernst; *An Essay on Man*; 237 p.; 1944; $1.75; Coll. Cassirer's famous essay on culture. Analysis of language, myth, art, religion, history and science with consideration of important theories and philosophies which relate to these fields.